The Billboard

The Billboard

How a lonely New Yorker hatched an idea that traveled
the globe and won him not just a wife, but a family

Tom Barrella

ISBN: 0692456066
ISBN 13: 9780692456064
Library of Congress Control Number: 2015908372
Abaco Press, Massapequa, NY

To my feisty wife, Sueli, whom I love dearly. To her precious daughters, Audrey and Isabelle, who have become my daughters. Also to my parents, Sally and Tom, for their unwavering support.

Contents

Preface

Our story begins with a man who seemingly exhausted all ways of finding a woman to whom he could give himself. He tried speed dating and went on blind dates. He traveled, walked, climbed, kayaked, and snorkeled with his dates. He found joy and sorrow and hope and heartbreak—just never a mate.

One particular dating site he frequented matched prospective dates and notified both the man and woman who it thought were matched well. Logging into the site one evening, he found two such notices. Two were better than no notices, but it was all for naught. One woman had already indicated her lack of interest, citing the unmanageable distance between them. But she lived on the north shore of Long Island's Nassau County, and he lived on the south shore. What was the time between them? It was only about forty minutes. What was the other woman's story? She, too, claimed to be uninterested because of the age difference between them. When he read that she was just three years younger than he was, he let out a primal scream and knew he'd finally had enough!

There just had to be a better way. Having just finished building his dream home, he was well past ready to settle down. He'd been successful in other areas of life. What was his intellect for if not to solve this most vexing of problems? He knew he had to do something unorthodox—something outrageous.

Perhaps he could hire a plane to fly along the beach, trailing a banner that proclaimed his availability. Or should he utilize skywriters, a hot-air balloon, a radio ad, or something else for that purpose? Perhaps "outrageous" equated to promoting himself on a billboard along a busy thoroughfare.

In the end, a billboard won out. It would be a huge billboard, twenty by sixty feet, located just outside the Manhattan Midtown Tunnel on the Long Island Expressway. It would feature only his silhouette accompanied by the simple message: see-tom.com.

The twenty-by-sixty-foot board outside the Midtown Tunnel.

Chapter 1

SEE TOM

Is there any way not to seem self-absorbed when describing oneself? Nowadays we are all told that we are special, gifted, or especially worthy. But the vast majority of us aren't. Popular culture is filled with these obnoxious, no-talent, pseudocelebrities who inexplicably prolong their fifteen minutes of fame to fifteen years. Could I possibly promote myself while maintaining some modesty? I had to try.

If I have a distinguishing characteristic, it would have to be that I have been gifted with both right- and left-brained qualities in the extreme. I can analyze a spreadsheet with the best of them, but I also have a creative drive that won't quit. The right side has suffered more than its share of assaults. In a quest to make sense of my life, I also learned that psychology considers me *highly sensitive*. That might come as a surprise to those who know me.

In the spring of my fortieth year, I did not let my free time go to waste. A great friend named Paul had set up shop in Fort Lauderdale and at times I'd keep a boat there under his watchful eye. I flew out of LaGuardia to visit him for one of our "road trips" around the Bahamas. Their small Bimini islands, so close to the US mainland, are just heaven on earth. Their blue-green waters are a powerful antidote to stress.

The day of the flight was also my deadline for committing to renting the billboard for the month of July. I went back and forth between having the courage to proceed and talking myself out of it. I'd made some serious money, but looking at the cost gave me pause.[1] It was time to fish or cut bait. I manned up, signed the contract, and sent it in along with a check for $20,000. Before I stepped on that flight, I was committed! It did wonders to focus my mind.

Wheels up and tray table down, I pulled out a pad and pen and used the few hours on the plane to sketch out what see-tom.com should look like. What emerged was a vision for a site that would be as playful as it was informative. There would be "Dress Tom," where women could test-drive several looks on me, from formal wear to beach

---

1 More than one person who wrote me after learning my story pointed out that for what I spent on the billboard and website, I could have bought an awful lot of private rooms, champagne, and prostitutes.

casual. It was one of the features that would give women a reason to stay awhile.[2]

Taking this a step further would be "Undress Tom." Here, I'd be shown dressed for the most extreme weather possible, with layer upon layer of coats, hats, scarves, and gloves. When a visitor clicked the "Undress Tom" button, an article of outer clothing would come off. If the woman clicked the button repeatedly in rapid succession, a message would pop up declaring, "Perv!" or pleading, "Please, I don't even know you!"

2 The site developers did an amazing job, going above and beyond what they'd promised. They thought it would be fun to insert a long denim skirt as one of the bottoms to try on me. Just to recognize their hard work and not wanting to be a buzzkill, I agreed to leave it in there. Doing so was a big mistake. While the site was up, I kept receiving suggestions that perhaps it wasn't a woman I was looking for.

As the number of clothing articles dwindled, a message would appear asking if the visitor was of legal age. Eventually, I'd be down to my boxers, with a very anxious look on my face. The "Undress Tom" button would turn red and begin to flash, "Warning!" If the person insisted on clicking it the final time, the boxers would be replaced by a small circular badge proclaiming, "I like your style. Call me!"[3]

There's always time for a good story, no? Over the years, I've been blessed to be able to get around and accumulate my share of experiences. The "Know Tom" section would be a collection of my stories. There was the time when out in the open ocean, returning from Bimini to Fort Lauderdale, Paul and I spotted this huge plume of roiling white water off in the distance. We couldn't figure out what it was. Over the next few minutes, it drew closer. We began to hear a captain calling out over the radio for a vessel heading in the direction we were heading. I picked up the mic and responded. He was indeed hailing us. He explained that we were on a collision course with him, and, since he was in a partially submerged US Navy submarine, he suggested that it might be a good idea for us to change course immediately. We did.

Let's go back a little further. As the head of my fraternity during college, I was aware that one of our pledges had a heart condition. We never made him do anything strenuous and generally took our cues from him as to whether any pledging activities could be an issue for him. The

---

3 While I was dying to have this feature in the site, the fact that I was a teacher gave me pause. In the end, I chickened out. "Undress Tom" never saw the light of day.

culmination of the pledging period was a walk from campus to the fraternity house. The brothers would meet the pledge class somewhere in the middle and let them know that when they arrived at the house they would be made brothers. The pledges get so excited that pledging was finally over that they usually picked up the pace. The pledge in question began jogging along with his class. When they all made it to the house, they gathered in the foyer. Moments later, the pledge in question collapsed.

This wasn't your garden-variety fainting; we couldn't find a pulse. I wondered, "Manslaughter? Negligent homicide?" All the promise I held was about to go down the tubes. I had the biggest guy in the fraternity carry the pledge to my car, and the three of us raced to the hospital. We never even made it to hospital. He regained consciousness on the way there.

To encourage women to tap into any lingering hostility toward men from their last break-ups, I envisioned your basic Whac-A-Mole game. But my head rather than that of a mole would pop out of the holes. If I was successfully whacked, stars would fly, and my smiling face would turn to a frown, my glasses would go all askew, and the player would score points.

While in Florida, I tossed around a bunch of ideas with Paul and another friend, Bill. After returning to Long Island, I was fortunate to find, without too much research, a web developer close to me on Long Island whose owner Ken was jazzed by what I was planning to do and who really embraced the challenge. All of the development on the site had to be done during May and June. The billboard was going up on July 1, ready or not.

After brainstorming sessions with the developer and his team, everybody was fired up. I realized that I had a lot of work to do. No photos had been taken and no stories written. For the next two months, I'd have to spend all my free time writing up those fond memories. A great photographer friend Tom and his wife Nancy came over to my house and invested a day taking all the "Dress Tom" shots. The developer took the Whac-A-Mole idea and turned it into "Bop Tom."[4] Each game lasted thirty seconds, and a score of twenty or higher was quite good. Things were coming together! And that June I turned forty-one.

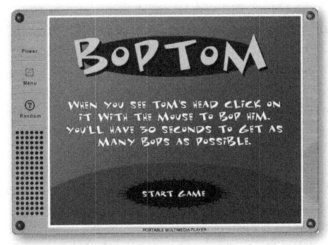

---

4 They did a great job implementing the game, but they had named it "Kill Tom." I tried as tactfully as I knew how to suggest that maybe conjuring death wasn't the best idea. In the end, I came up with the more innocuous "Bop Tom."

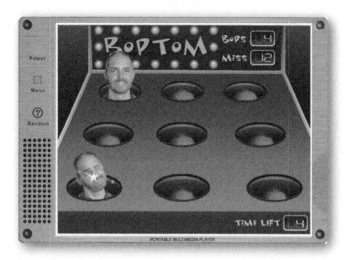

It just so happened that the website developer also employed a public-relations team. He suggested that I think about getting the word out to the press about what I was doing. The billboard would be its own promotion, but significant press coverage would be an enormous bonus. "Good idea. Let's do it," I said. We needed an interesting angle, and the team came up with it. At the end of June we distributed a press release entitled, "Man Plans to Create His Own Fireworks This July Fourth!"

Chapter 2

It's On!

On July 1 I got a call from an excited PR person. The *New York Daily News* dedicated all of page three to a story it titled "TOM'S COM-ON FOR A WIFE— TRYING BILLBOARD, WEBSITE." The paper's website did even better, with my picture smack-dab in the middle of the home page the whole day. I couldn't ask for a better start![5]

---

5 Soon after the billboard appeared, up popped an online thread of bloggers who believed that "Tom" would later be revealed as a corporate marketing campaign and that I was just an actor in this plan.

Then, CBS New York's evening news did a story on my quest, visiting the website and highlighting its more creative aspects as well as the billboard. The anchors had a good chuckle over the irreverant parts of the site.[6]

Next, I was invited for an interview on NBC's *Today*. That was an experience. I was led out to an awkwardly shaped, three-foot-deep couch just seconds before we went live. I didn't immediately find a way to sit comfortably, and, the next thing I knew, we were live, and I was answering questions from host Natalie Morales.[7]

---

6 Strangely enough, my brother also made the same broadcast, but for a more mundane reason: He had just undergone a new sinus procedure.

7 To this day it pisses me off, because I got e-mails telling me that I sat like a girl. I am sure there were plenty of people who took one look and shouted at their TVs, "No wonder you're single! Who sits like that?"

The Billboard

During a visit to the website developer a day later, I met with two women: the PR person and the assistant who'd accompanied me to *Today*. We'd equipped the site with a contact page that forwarded each inquiry to me as an e-mail. But I was too nervous to log in and check the account. Now, with one of the women looking over each of my shoulders, I logged into the e-mail account for the first time. High fives ensued all around as we saw dozens of e-mails filling up the inbox! Hope was high that among them was the future Mrs. Barrella. All of our hard work was paying off!

I had designed the "Contact Tom" form to be an indication of what I like in a woman. Getting past the preliminaries like age, height, and weight, I developed an "I am/I have" area in which I identified a host of traits that I found attractive in a woman, as follows:

I am: (check all that apply) adventurous, informed, classy, sensitive, fit, passionate, inquisitive, feminine, gracious, talkative, accomplished, spiritual, intelligent, genuine, creative, introspective, irreverent, energetic

I have: (check all that apply) personality, humility, vitality, my sea legs, decency, integrity, a sense of humor, an opinion, style

Next were three quotations about love. I asked that each woman choose the one that meant the most to her and a reason for her choice. (I'm a teacher, so I find it critical to ask why.) The quotations were:

- Love is strong yet delicate. It can be broken. To truly love is to understand this. To be in love is to respect this.
- If I am pressed to say why I loved him, I feel it can only be explained by replying, "Because it was he; because it was me."
- Marriage is not a ritual or an end. It is a long, intricate, intimate dance together, and nothing matters more than your own sense of balance and your choice of partner.

The Contact Tom form finished with a place for women to write anything they wanted me to know as well as how I could contact them. In hindsight, it might have felt like a job application to some. On the positive side, it certainly acted as a screen to eliminate the women who would contact me as a goof.

OK, so the three of us were there at the developer's office, huddling around a monitor showing an in-box full of inquiries. We held our collective breath as I clicked on the first one. Up popped a profile of a woman who was not exactly my type, but whose story and sincerity I really appreciated. We tried the second. Again, she was not who I had envisioned, but there were many profiles waiting. Over the next several minutes, two led to five led to twenty. With each passing contact, my heart sank a bit farther. Wanting to have children, I was hoping to be contacted by women my age or younger. Instead, many were older—much older. I'm five feet ten and 160 pounds "soaking wet," as my dad likes to say. Some of these women were really, really big. One sent a picture of herself in front of a bedroom door, I think. I say "I think" because I couldn't see the door.

At that moment I realized just how much time, money, energy, and, most importantly, hope I'd invested in finding the love of a lifetime. I'd been on a high for months, loving the creative process, watching my vision for the site become a reality, and hoping that, by putting myself out there, something wonderful just might happen for me. Suddenly it became clear that I had just been kidding myself. The PR women who were sitting expectantly at the edges of their seats just a few minutes earlier were speechless. It didn't take much to notice that I was crushed. I could see that they didn't know what to say, so we all just sat there in silence.

I left the office completely deflated, but I reminded myself that it was still early in the month of July. There were many more media outlets to contact about my story. More exposure would lead to more inquires. Still, it would be difficult to swing back to the euphoria of our early media coverage from the disillusionment with the results it was now producing.

Scoring an interview on *Today* was a pretty big deal, but we landed an even bigger fish in *The View*. To set up my appearance, the producers wanted to show the audience a taped segment that provided the backstory. We met the film crew at the base of the billboard in Long Island City.

I fumbled and tripped on every line possible. The idea was for me to explain that I'd had enough of being single and that I'd decided to do this…(I then would turn and look up while their camera pulled back to reveal the billboard behind me). We eventually moved to their offices, where I sat at a desk and explained what awaited women who decided they wanted to see Tom. We spent hours filming, because I was so nervous I just couldn't get a sentence out. I've never been a good promoter of myself, and it showed. We eventually got enough footage for them to put together a decent segment.

Before I knew it, I was going through makeup and then making small talk with the other guests in the green room. The whole thing was surreal. During a commercial break, they walked me out onto the set and sat me at a curved table in the middle of Meredith Vieira, Star Jones, Joy Behar, and Elisabeth Hasselbeck. At least I thought that was what was happening. I've never before or since had the feeling of being invisible as I had at that moment. The panel did nothing to acknowledge my presence.

If someone whom you were about to interview was just seated next to you, wouldn't you look over and at least smile? Would you make eye contact or somehow acknowledge his or her presence? These women did not; whatever conversation they were having prior to my taking a seat continued uninterrupted. I think it was Star on one side of me talking to Joy on the other side about what each was planning to do that weekend. I did some quick geometry and concluded that, to continue conversing with each other, they had to look through me! It was bizarre.

It's On!

For whatever reason, when we went live, I was, as ESPN's Stuart Scott liked to say, "cool like the other side of the pillow." Each of the hosts had been fed a question for me on an index card. One asked if I hadn't gone overboard spending so much money trying to find a mate. I said that money was an enabler, and if it helped me to find someone as important as a wife, then the investment would be well worth it. Joy noted that I said that I was looking for women in their thirties even though I was in my forties. I wondered if she chose this buzzkill question herself. I acknowledged that this was true, but I also opined that (obviously) women could decide for themselves whether I was age-appropriate. Several friends and family members were watching from home. Later in the day, my ordinarily relaxed sister-in-law Sue called to give me props about my appearance. About Joy's question, she proclaimed, "That bitch!"

To my appearance on *The View*, I can add a Fox cable show whose name escapes me as well as several radio interviews from as far away as New Zealand. Then there was the local network that sent a reporter and satellite truck to my parents' home. They explained that I didn't live there. They refused to give the reporter my address, at which point he said that if he couldn't interview me that day, then he wasn't going to do the story. It's just as well. Is there anything more obnoxious than having a reporter show up, knock, and shove a microphone into someone's face as soon as he or she opens the door? Or maybe it would have been a "through-the-screen-door" interview, which commonly takes place with the next-door neighbor of a man who has been hiding some awful secret, like dead bodies in the basement. My parents stayed mum, and the interview never happened.

Chapter 3

LIVING THE LIFE

Thankfully, the media exposure I'd received resulted in several hundred women writing. A small percentage (i.e., the women who appealed to me) of a big number can still be a big number. But, like someone trying to drink through a fire hose, I was in trouble from the beginning. Let's say that as few as ten of the women who wrote me really intrigued me. What was I to do next: Contact all of them to ensure that they don't lose interest, and then string them along? Or contact a few so I don't overload my ability give them each time? I hadn't thought this through beforehand, but I am not confident that I would have come up with a good solution anyhow.

My living situation at the time was "off the hook." I had just finished designing and building the "Big Blue House," a huge canal-front colonial on Long Island's south shore.

Friends, family, and neighbors wondered why a single guy would build such a big place. My response was, "If you build it, they—a wife and kids—will come."

The seawall was also completely new, as were dockside electric and water service and a thirty-foot floating dock that would be home to a beautiful, thirty-foot express cruiser (i.e., a boat).[8] Additional toys included a motorized dinghy and two-person kayak. I was a teacher who was off for the summer. Was I ever ready for a memorable summer! Not wanting to fall victim to analysis paralysis, I picked up the phone, called a few women, and just went with it.

I considered what it meant if a woman would rather venture into the choppy Great South Bay in a kayak than glide over it on the boat. Certainly, she'd be saltier, more adventurous, and willing to get a little wet in order to be closer to nature. The kayak was also a great way to see if we'd be able to work as a team (or just paddle around in circles).

That kayak proved to be a lot of fun. It could be paddled right up into the marshes that dotted the middle of the bay. We could grab mussels off the reeds without even leaving the thing. If we chose to get out and walk around, we could also clam. Then there was the crab "hotel" I left hanging from the dock most nights. It landed so many blue claws that with each batch I'd try a different way of preparing them.

---

8 The dock was covered with a long-lasting, non-splintering species of Brazilian wood called IPE that I was told was so hard and so dense that it doesn't float. I didn't believe the dock builder, so I took a small piece and dropped it in a bucket of water. It sank.

At first, I dated women from the local area who had written. But after a tall, blond Floridian drink of water showed up on the radar, the local dating thing became more of a guideline than a rule. She'd seen me on TV, loved my out-of-the-box thinking, and opined that I didn't look half bad. The following Saturday she'd be flying up and basically going right past me on her way to a charity event in the Hamptons. "Nice," I thought. Long story short, she flew in on a Friday morning—a perfect day—and hopped on a Long Island Rail Road (LIRR) train going east. I met her at my stop at eleven o'clock. As she walked off the plat-form, I left my car and walked toward her. We greeted each other with sly smiles. In a few minutes, we were back at my home and hopping on the boat to head for a lunch in Freeport. As the closest town to an inlet (access to the ocean), Freeport still has a commercial fishing industry. However, it's best known for its "Nautical Mile" of res-taurants, bars, and shops that are jumping in the summer. Robin took a seat beside me at the helm. As we pulled away from the dock, I cracked open a beverage for each of us. We toasted the sun, the warm breeze, and our unlikely date.

The ride over to Freeport couldn't have been more picturesque. The boating channel meandered its way around the reedy islands dotting the bay. It swept under the Wantagh and Meadowbrook parkways that, come sum-mer, bring millions of visitors to Jones Beach. Everywhere we looked the sun was glistening off the water. We ex-changed knowing nods with the captains of passing vessels to confirm that we boaters got to experience something special.

In a half-hour we arrived at the canal that runs along the Nautical Mile. Throttling back the engines to idle speed, we made our way up the canal. Moments later we pulled up to a popular spot called Bracco's Clam and Oyster Bar. Boat handling in tight quarters is not for the faint of heart. The current can be going one way while the wind, a completely independent and powerful force, can be blowing in another direction. And how significant a force the wind applies to a boat depends on what direction the boat is pointing. A boat pointing into or away from the wind presents less surface area to push than a boat that is broadside to the wind. In order to position the boat for an approach to a dock, it's often necessary to rotate the boat and thereby expose it to the wind's varying influence.

The fiberglass that most boats are made of doesn't like to flex when struck with any appreciable force. Its preferred method of absorbing a significant blow is to crack. Other boat owners don't take kindly to your boat colliding with theirs while you're trying to secure yours in an adjacent slip. To top it off, on a sunny summer day there is a patio full of restaurant patrons keeping an eye on approaching boats if for no other reason than to get a little free entertainment. But this day restaurant-goers would just have to get their thrills elsewhere. I docked the boat without incident. Arriving at a restaurant by water makes a nice entrance.

Disembarking while accompanied by Ms. Florida Sunshine in tow was nicer.

Soaking in the sun at our seaside table, Robin and I ordered some light fare and tall drinks. We talked, laughed, and joked. We were both so relaxed and happy that we'd just look at each other and smile. We'd stolen an unlikely moment from our ordinary lives and were fully intent on savoring it. Perhaps if we hadn't acknowledged the passage of time, it would have stood still. But at some point, reality beckons. The sun begins its slow descent. The waitress looks at you with a polite smile. We reluctantly agreed to pull ourselves away. Robin had a train to catch, and I had a different sort of problem. It was five o'clock. Our lovely four-hour lunch lasted quite a bit longer than I imagined it would have when I'd made a date for dinner with another woman for six o'clock at the Nautilus Café—in Freeport!

I hustled the boat back across the bay. After docking at the house we jumped in the car, and I shuttled Robin to the train station. Wanting to end the date the right way, I waited with Robin on the station platform to ensure she got on the correct train. As it pulled in, we shared a bittersweet moment. She lived in Florida, and I lived in New York. Did our mutual ease mean we were right for each other, or did we just catch lightning in a bottle? With a hug, a kiss, and a smile, she stepped onto her train. As its doors closed and it pulled out of sight, I switched up from a poignant wave to tear-assing down the stairs and into my car. I raced down Sunrise Highway toward Freeport. The trip is a lot shorter via car, but, when you're late, the traffic-light gods know it. Some twenty minutes later, I pulled into the Nautilus's parking lot and tried to compose myself as I entered. Despite the fact that I'd gotten a few text messages out to Teresa over the last hour that I was running late, I found her stewing at the bar. After all, it was a perfect day, there were no accidents or road construction or anything to justify my lateness, and, heck, I was off for the summer. How the hell could I not make a six o'clock dinner date? I was forty-five minutes late.

Teresa was an accomplished woman. When she contacted me via the site, she expressed a traditionalist's view of dating and wanted the man to be creative in romance. The only thing I was going to be creative about was my excuse for being so late. Alas, no number of apologies or amount of small talk was going to change her mood or mind about me. Talk about a tale of two dates, and on the same day!

Mention Brazil, and Americans are most likely to think of the mighty Amazon, the annual Carnival, or the soaring statue of Jesus Christ that presides over Rio de Janeiro. But there is so much more to this melting pot of more than two hundred million. As the United States dominates North America, Brazil dominates South America. Within its borders sits nearly half the land mass of South

America. Its economy is the world's seventh largest. Beaches? Mountains? Canyons? Waterfalls? Rain forests? Brazil has them all. But what makes Brazil so special are the people. Warm and gracious, Brazilians have a certain "joie de vivre" that powers them through literally hours of nonstop dancing and celebration at Carnival. Try dancing the samba for five minutes, and you will see how exhausting it can be.

Among Brazil's—indeed the world's—largest broadcasters is TV Globo. During the summer of See Tom, the network was working on a special about what single people do to find a mate. Globo's New York City office learned about me and thought what I was doing would make an interesting addition to its broadcast. In the middle of July, it arranged to have its people spend a morning interviewing me in Lower Manhattan's Washington Square Park, to be followed by a drive out to my home on Long Island to observe me in my natural habitat. When we arrived, I proudly gave the crew the grand tour. I demonstrated the gee-whiz, pop-up downdraft vent behind the cooktop on the kitchen island and the floor-level vacuum-powered dust tray. The crew showed me how to make the famous Brazilian Caipirinha drink. In fact, before arriving at the house, we had stopped by the grocery store to make sure we would have all the ingredients conveniently at hand. This refreshing concoction features squeezed limes, sugar, "cachaca," (loosely described as Brazilian vodka) and crushed ice shaken with all the vigor one can muster.

The Billboard

After toasting the camera, we ventured upstairs because the crew had asked me if I'd go through some of my daily routines. With the camera still rolling, I demonstrated my ironing prowess. After I changed clothes, I sat at my universal weight machine and, pushing my chest out as far as it would go, knocked out a few reps. So much for leaving them wanting more. Having nothing else to possibly document, the crew left shortly afterward.

I spent my midsummer days mostly responding to inquiries via e-mail. I'd made a pledge to write to every woman who'd taken the time to write me. It was an honor to read the highly personal and poignant stories these women wanted to share with me. There were two things we all had in common: how much we wanted to find someone special and how much energy we had expended in our pursuits. Their honesty was refreshing and invigorating. They deserved my best in return.[9]

When I wasn't writing, I was dating. One woman I dated, Karen, was an irreverent beauty with lustrous brown hair and dark brown eyes, who lived right there on Long Island. She came over to the house for several home-caught crab meals. We'd have some wine, and then, when we decided to eat, I'd get a big pot, fill it with a small amount of water, and drop in a strainer. I experimented with seasoning the water with everything from

---

9 In the end, I did not follow through on my pledge. Having been written by over a thousand English-writing women alone (i.e., excluding the Brazilians), I only responded to about three hundred of the women.

lemon juice to beer to Old Bay seasoning. After bringing the water to a boil, I would toss in several good-sized and vibrantly colored blue-claw crabs that had checked into the hotel I'd lowered to the bottom of the canal. My weapon of choice was a pair of salad tongs. I would move the tongs toward a crab, intending to close them around its upper and lower body, but the critter would have none of it. It would defend itself by grabbing the tong's arms with both claws. There was no way to approach a crab from behind because it would always maneuver to face you, its beady little eyes trained on you. Once I finally secured one in the tongs, I'd move it over the pot with the intent of dropping it in. I'd open the tongs, at which point the crab would continue to hold on tightly, staring at me with contempt. Or it would not grab the tongs but would fully spread out and stiffen its arms and legs so that it wouldn't fit into the pot. Even when it seemed I had the upper hand and that victory was near, a crab would actually grab the rim of pot on the way down. The whole experience was surreal.[10]

When I eventually got as many in there as we were going to eat, I'd drop the lid and turn on the burner. That's when things went to a whole new level. As the water rapidly heated up, the crabs would go ballistic, scampering around and banging the inside of the pot while trying to

---

10 I had to do some research on blue claws. One fact I found comforting is that their life-span is just three years. I also concluded that the large size of the crabs meant that they were a lot closer to the end of their lives than the beginning.

get out. It was a shocking and macabre scene; I would not recommend it as a precursor to romance. But I noticed that Karen watched with (could it be?) excitement as the scene unfolded. After her inquiring about our doing the "crab thing" one too many evenings, I thought it might be best to move on.[11]

The highlight of the last few summers leading up to and including See Tom was a week-long tuna-fishing trip off Ocean City, Maryland. Paul, Bill (who lived nearby, in Baltimore), and I made a good team. Paul was the angler, bringing his skills and equipment to the party. I brought the boat and ability to get us to and from the fishing grounds. This was not a trivial undertaking, as the best fishing was found forty miles off shore. When we got a fish near the boat, I'd be at the helm maneuvering the boat so that the line would avoid the propellers. Bill did everything else, perhaps the most important of which was gaffing the tuna that we got to the boat.

On several trips, Paul and I had been able to bring our dads along. Having raised families for two decades in adjacent homes, our fathers bickered more like spouses than friends did. But to give them the thrill of fishing for a big catch was well worth our putting up with the chatter. Plus, they were both old fishing hands who could fillet the heck out of fish. This skill would come

---

11 I've since developed a more humane way to steam crabs (or at least I think it's more humane). By placing them in icy water they go dormant. Presumably, they don't know what's going to happen next.

in handy over the course of our trips, as the tuna counts swelled.

The first part of such a trip involved getting down there from Long Island. It's exactly 153 nautical miles between the buoys marking the Jones Beach and the Ocean City inlets. For my boat *School's Out*, a thirty-one-foot express cruiser made by Chaparral, that's an eight-hour nonstop ride in good sea conditions. Poor conditions not only meant a longer trip, but a slower, very fuel-inefficient speed. Given the fuel capacity, poor conditions meant the trip could not be made nonstop. Any time we were in doubt, we would duck into the inlet at Atlantic City, New Jersey, for fuel.

While there were several marinas in the Ocean City, Maryland, area, we'd always stayed at the Ocean City Fishing Center and found the staff to be friendly, helpful, and downright funny. With a great bar and small army of charter fishing boats, there's always something going on there.

Fishing off an "express cruiser," a recreational boat designed to seat a crowd, is a challenge akin to moving a loveseat by tying it to the top of the family sedan. It might work, but it'll draw concerned looks from all over. The boats that normally ply the waters are fifty-foot or longer "sport fishers" that are hired out (with captain and crew) by weekend warriors. These expensive, heavy-duty, purpose-built boats are designed to split the water as they move forward.

My thirty-footer (in white with black canvas) dwarfed by
a custom fishing boat, which sits in the next slip.

An express cruiser is designed mostly to skip over
the water. On days when the wind was faint, we would
glide past the fleet on the magic carpet of calm seas. But
when the conditions were snotty, even at low speeds we'd
bounce all over the place while others muscled their $1-
and $2-million battle wagons past us. I'd walk the fine line,
getting us to and from at a rate of speed just short of that
necessary to tear the boat apart. Over the years there had
been a few days when we'd cried uncle and, on the return
ride, slipped behind one of the monsters to benefit from
its wave-crushing abilities. The closer one stays to the wake

of one of these boats, the calmer the water. But in an open ocean, it's not nice to run up the back of another boat, and so, I always worked to remain a reasonable distance behind. The crews of the sport fishers would occasionally glance back at us. We wondered whether their general impression was closer to "those are some ballsy guys to be out here in these seas in that boat" or "what a bunch of dumb asses." However, we didn't become pre-occupied with what others thought. In fishing there is one sure-fire way to earn respect: catch fish. We caught a lot of fish.

Over a week-long trip, we would take some time off to recharge. The Ocean City boardwalk was a popular place to kill a few hours. During the See-Tom summer, we were on the boardwalk and noticed an Internet café. Paul and I slipped in to check our e-mail and see what was going on in the world. At the computer, I jumped out of my seat, and Paul eyed me quizzically. "Wow," I blurted out. "The Brazilian station must have run the piece they were doing on me. I have four hundred inquiries from Brazilian women in my account!" Major high-fives were in order as we held a two-man celebration. Many of my crazier stories were made possible by Paul's friendship and adventurous nature, so it was fitting that he'd been there at that moment.

A less dynamic area of the See-Tom site was a page of personal references. Several longtime friends had agreed to write fairly lengthy missives on how great a guy I was. All but one was written by women, which hopefully would put female visitors at ease. Even though they didn't know each other, these friends managed to write the same thing: "If my husband died and I married Tom, my husband would be happy for me."

Paul's reference was a hilarious commentary on our conflicting paths to adulthood. Growing up, he hung with the wrong crowd, partied early and often, and was on a first-name basis with the school principal. Always enterprising, on hot summer days Paul would take his boat and a massive cooler around the coves in Oyster Bay to sell ice cream to boaters at anchor. By the time he moved up to high school, Paul had developed a tee-shirt-printing business. One memorable run-in with our high school's administration was over a collegiate-themed shirt that was increasingly seen in the halls: Drunken State. The point of Paul's personal remarks on my site was that his lifetime of having fun and my lifetime of work and sacrifice had gotten us to the same place.

Back at the Internet café, nothing more needed to be said. Paul rolled his chair over and leaned forward as we began to look at the responses. In general, the Brazilian women were younger than the women in the stateside responses. We quickly realized that it would take forever to put a dent in this pile and that cursory looks wouldn't do these women justice. The trip would be over in a few days. They would have to wait.

Our week of fishing was a major success. Chasing and catching tuna that weighed forty to one hundred pounds or more meant hundreds of pounds of tuna meat. Oh, sure, you've got your tuna steaks, tuna sandwiches, tuna pâté, and tuna salad, but there's only so much tuna that four guys can eat in a week.

Paul's dad, Marty; Paul's girlfriend; Paul; my dad, Tom; and me

My dad, Tom, and Paul's dad, Marty, were old filleting hands.

I'd thought ahead and brought an "As Seen on TV" vacuum sealer. We could fit two extra-thick steaks in each bag. After returning to port each day, we'd fillet what we'd caught, vacuum-seal the bags, and give them to the dock-master for storage in the marina's walk-in freezer. At the end of the trip, we laid out dozens of packages of frozen tuna and divvied them up. At some point in the process, Paul's dad, Marty, declared, "I want a choice piece!" to which my dad replied in exasperation, "Marty, they're all choice pieces!"

One of the things I'd planned in the Big Blue House was a home theater whose screen could double as a computer monitor. The Panasonic fifty-inch HD-plasma screen that hung over the fireplace was the real deal for its time. A few button-presses on the remote and a tap of the wireless keyboard to wake up the computer would allow me to kick back and surf the web from the comfort of my couch.

Upon my return home, my friend John stopped by to hear about the trip. One afternoon we sat down in the sun-drenched den where I showed him a bunch of fishing photos on the big screen. While we talked, I logged into my e-mail account and clicked on the profile of the first Brazilian woman to contact me. Her smiling face appeared. John gave her the once-over. I clicked "Next," and then, a few moments later, "Next" again. John asked who these women were.

"Brazilian ladies wanting to meet me," I replied.

"How many?"

"At this point, it's up to seven hundred."

John stood up and started pacing and shaking his head as he wrestled to come to grips with the situation. "You've just built your dream house on the water. You've got an awesome boat. You're a teacher who's off for the summer. You just returned from an amazing fishing trip. Now you have hundreds of Brazilian women wanting to meet you! What could be better?"

"Being fluent in Portuguese, for starters." Having scanned many of these new inquiries, I was very disappointed to see that nearly all of the women wrote me in their native language. Sure, I could make out some of the passages. There were many sentences like "Tenho 26 anos," which I figured was "I have twenty-six years." So let's review: I was a continent apart, a language apart, and, based on the number of twenty-somethings in my inbox, nearly a generation apart from the Brazilians. Unlike countries such as Germany, Brazil does not mandate that its students learn English as a second language. Damn the Brazilian education system!

Of course, they say the language of love is universal and primal: you woman; me man. Having to teach each other how to speak our respective languages could be enticing. For now, I could make use of translate.com. I could pop their passages into the window and see English versions of what the women wrote. The translations wouldn't have to be perfect, just good enough for me to get the gist. Still, I began to believe that, despite my rationalizing, this treasure trove of Brazilian beauties was substantially less, shall we say, actionable.

There had to be a better way. I contacted the producers at TV Globo in Manhattan and buttered them up with the news that their segment on me had motivated hundreds of Brazilian lovelies to write. They were wowed. Then I pitched them my idea:

> I would give them the names of the women whom I most wanted to meet. They would fly me to Rio for a week and fly in the women from around Brazil as well. I would stay seven nights and have seven dates. It would be on their dime, and they could roll tape the whole time.

They were gaga over the idea. We discussed the logistics of me getting down there before school started up in early September. It would be a little tight, but we could make it work. I immediately went online and found a local school for Portuguese and …Let's stop here. The Rio thing didn't happen. It's something that only now occurred to me.

If a face can launch a thousand ships, it can certainly drive one man to distraction. Among the seven hundred was one whose freshness was so arresting that she could have brightened up a toothpaste commercial. For those in my generation, she conjured up visions of Phoebe Cates in *Fast Times at Ridgemont High*. For the Millennials, maybe a mix of Ariana Grande and Selena Gomez? The bottom line is that this woman's beauty had me punching like a prizefighter against the language barrier.

So I wrote a blurb on translate.com, translated it, and pasted the conversion into an e-mail to her. I received a response in English. I had asked her if there was a chance she spoke English, and she answered in the affirmative. Yes! But something just wasn't right. For example, I'd write an e-mail telling her something about my family. She'd reply with "He shares himself with others. It is nice to know him." I thought, "Either (a) this woman was instructed by the worst English teacher on the planet, (b) she was fibbing when she told me she spoke English and is using the worst translator to cover for it, or (c) she's not referring to me but instead to our Lord Jesus Christ." The front-runner was (b).

I could manage being referred to in the third person. But soon I began to notice that at the bottom of her e-mails, she'd slipped in a link. I clicked it once and retrieved an article, in English, on the redeeming power of God. This woman wanted to share her love of God with me. That was powerful stuff, but, oddly, she never specifically addressed her love of God when she wrote. I'd gently ask her what she was hoping for by including the links; I wondered if part of her church's plan was to have each member convert, say, one person on each continent. I never did get an answer I could understand. Soon, instead of including a link at the bottom of an e-mail, she'd save me a click by copying an article from its source and pasting it into her e-mail—images and all. Fast forward a few e-mails, and I would start to see multiple, successive articles copied in. After what seemed like just a few more e-mails, she copied the entire contents of the faith's website into her e-mail. OK then—it was time to move on.

I was not exaggerating about the Portuguese language barrier. A thorough review of my seeming Brazilian riches yielded ten—ten!—women writing me in English. Nearly all of these had spent some time in the United States. I wrote to several of them. One just wanted a pen pal with whom she could practice her English. She wasn't interested in a long-distance relationship, but she knew a few women in New York with whom she could set me up. Another happened to be living in California. She was young, beautiful, and fluent in English. Who knows what happened with her.

Almost as soon as my adventure began, it seemed to be drawing to a close. As July neared its end, so did the days that my billboard would proudly greet eastbound travelers on the Long Island Expressway. Not that I was looking to spend any more money, but I did make a quick phone call to the billboard company to ask whether it was even possible to extend it through the month of August. No dice—the rep coolly replied that it was under contract for August. But while he had me on the phone, he asked what I wanted to do with the massive sheet of vinyl when they took it down. I didn't know there was an option. Perhaps they could drop it by helicopter onto the roof of my house, making it visible to passing air traffic. With a tinge of sadness, I told them to trash it.

My attempt to drink from a fire hose had nearly drowned me. In a short period of time, I had all these women interested in me. But conversations take time, dates take more time, and relationships, even more. I wasn't quite sure what to do next.

Chapter 4

PARTY'S OVER

And then it was over. Superintendent's Conference Day, the first day of the new school year, arrived in late August. It was with trepidation that I slipped into school that first day, wondering what the administration would think of my little adventure. While writing the stories and content for the site, I was very conscientious about playing everything straight. There was nothing on the website that could be even remotely construed as sexual, immoral, or profane. These omissions may have cost me some hot-to-trot women, but, whatever, I couldn't go there. Upon learning of the billboard and website, a few current and former students had contacted me over the summer. I imagined that the administration had pored over the site in search of inappropriate material. Of course, the first person I saw when I walked in the door was our veteran, old-school principal. He flashed a wry smile, quipping, "I heard that you had an interesting summer." His smile broadened. It was a big relief.

Superintendent's Conference Day, for teachers only, gives us a day to begin turning our minds around and getting ready for a new school year. I was a minor celebrity among my two-hundred-plus colleagues who had figured they'd wait for this day to get the skinny on my summer.[12]

While many teachers are able to maintain a significant distance between themselves and their students, that's just not my style. A colleague sums up how teachers should relate to students: "Friendly, not friends." While I am not the students' friend, I do want them to feel as though they have a personal relationship with me. I want to help them to develop empathy, have one non-parental adult in their lives with whom they can feel comfortable, and offer a modicum of stability.

I know it's hard for boys to sit still for seven hours a day—in fact, I think it's nauseating to expect them to. I find that if I can get them to like me, they work harder. And, truth be known, I want to have as much fun in a day as the kids. If a student who teeters on the back two legs of his chair falls on his butt, it's funny, and the kids are going to laugh. It's not brain surgery. At any given moment,

---

12 Some months after school resumed, one of my colleagues brought her young son to school. They were about to pass me in the hall when she stopped, pointed to me, and proclaimed to her son, "Look. It's Bop Tom!" He was wide-eyed and speechless, as if he'd met a superhero.

exactly nothing is at stake. We can always afford a few minutes for laughter.

Laura was a pen pal from Michigan whom I began communicating with over summer. We continued through the fall and winter. She confided that her best friend remained unconvinced that I was for real. To find out, they decided to fly to NYC for a weekend. I met them at a bar one night so the three of us could chat. Things went well enough that over the winter we began a long-distance relationship, alternating visits and spending time with each other's friends and family. Laura even flew down to Grand Bahama and met up with Paul, his girlfriend, and me there. Was it good? It was. But was it great? I guess not. At some point, she just went incommunicado.

As the days grew longer and warmer, I found myself back at square one. The approaching "summer after" promised to be a huge comedown. Just the thought of revisiting the list of women who'd written put me in a funk. I felt like a company that gets an inquiry on its website about a product shown there. A year later its rep calls the prospect and says, "If you remember, some time ago you contacted us about our product. Are you still interested?" "Ugh," I thought with a shudder.

Would I have to go back to the dating sites? I'd sworn them off in disgust. The details escape me, but somehow I found myself at a supposed networking event in Manhattan among a bunch of uncomfortable singles and couples. I distinctly remember approaching two women and introducing myself, which apparently was a big mistake. Not only was I not to their liking, but I was actually worthy of their contempt for even having the audacity to approach them. A spontaneous competition arose, with each one attempting to toss remarks more snide than the other. It was painful. That was the idea. I took the high road and walked away. The evening had barely begun and was already a disaster.

Given that my travel to the event consumed well over an hour, I took one long look at the assembled characters to decide if there was any reason to stay. As I scanned the room, one person clearly stood out. He was looking around cluelessly, not trying to be coy. Hadn't he seen *Zoolander*? He wasn't afraid of making and holding eye contact. I thought, "Screw it. May as well talk to this guy." Named Felipe, he was as friendly as I'd anticipated. His heavy accent made it obvious why he stood out. He was not from around here. Felipe explained that he'd taken a month off from work and decided to visit the United States to practice his English. As he explained how each night he would go out to a different bar and talk to women, a look of exasperation swept over his face. Apparently he'd been striking out four hours a night, every night—with one exception.

Felipe had actually come there that night with a woman. While she was in the powder room, he explained that she was tending bar at the place he visited the prior evening. When she befriended him, she asked if he'd accompany her to the networking event. I asked where he was from. "Brazil," he replied.

As a twenty-something professional beginning a career in banking and being helped along the way by a successful father, Felipe was in a good place in his life. Not too many people bum around Manhattan for a month to bone up on their English. The guy was friendly and funny. His lack of pretension was refreshing.

His English did need some work. We talked about interests. He said he liked the American movies that he identified as *Hockey* and *Hambow*. "*Hockey* and *Hambow*, *Hockey* and *Hambow*," I'm repeating to myself, trying to figure out what he means. "Ah, got it. Just slide in an *R* where he's using *H* and you get *Rocky* and *Rambo*!—Sly Stallone!" The pronunciation of the letter *r* became a long-running joke between us. Of course, it's easy to goof on someone trying to speak my native language. At least they're speaking it. The only language I'm fluent in is English.

Long story short, Felipe offered to host me if I wanted to visit him in São Paulo. Since it was the beginning of what promised to be a long summer, it was an offer I couldn't refuse. I made travel plans a couple of weeks out, visited the Brazilian consulate in Manhattan for a visa, and started reading up on Brazil. Now that I finally had a good reason to return to the list, I checked to see if there were any Brazilian women who'd written me in English from São Paulo. As Brazil's largest city by a wide margin, São Paulo was home to several. I wrote to let them know I was coming to town. One wrote back to tell me that she'd moved to the northern part of the country. Another would be out of the town during my visit there. One didn't reply. And one, my on-and-off Brazilian pen pal, said she was interested in meeting me.

The flight from JFK to São Paulo's Guarulhos Airport is nine hours. Thankfully, it's nearly due south of New York, so there's little change in time. During the non-day-light-savings portions of the year, São Paulo is only one hour ahead of the Eastern time zone within which New York sits. The cities being positioned on opposite sides of the equator means that our seasons are opposite each other. It also means that in the fall, when we set our clocks back an hour, São Paulo is moving forward an hour, which results in a time difference of three hours. Felipe's taking the month of July off to visit NYC occurred during his winter. A São Paulo winter can be rainy and chilly, but there is no snow.

Going and coming, travelers have the option of flying overnight or eating up a full day in the air. I opted for the latter and landed in the early evening. Felipe picked me up in his Jeep Cherokee, a luxury vehicle there. On the way back to his place, we noticed that something was amiss at a big intersection that was lit up like an operating room. Police cars were everywhere. As we crept toward the intersection, we were approached by two police officers on foot who, with guns drawn, were barking out orders. Having no idea what they were saying, I gave the universal symbol of cooperation: I put my hands where they could see 'em. The cops closed in on the car, gave the two of us the once-over, looked in the back to find nothing, and let us go our way. The traffic jam, police lights, and close encounter really rattled nerves. Later on, a car cut Felipe off, which caused him to brake hard to avoid a collision. He threw up his hands in disgust, yelling, "Go to the hell!"

Having just taken off work for a month, Felipe was not in a position to take yet more time off to run me around São Paulo. I'd planned my trip with this in mind by spanning two weekends over which he'd have more time to show me around. Felipe suggested that in the mornings I could walk to the social club he was a member of to have breakfast, work out, or even swim. He wrote up a short list of questions that would help me get in the place, order some food, and get out. It included *quanto custa?* for "what is the cost?" Sitting at the club restaurant on a weekday in winter at midmorning, I had the place nearly to myself. The menu was in Portuguese. Reaching back to my four years of high-school instruction in Latin-based Italian, I worked my way through several meals over several mornings. No chicken hearts or lamb's brains crossed my plate that I know of. Using my credit card allowed me to sidestep currency issues. The slogan is true: "Visa, it's everywhere you want to be."

In the evenings, we'd go out to dinner and then visit the local bars. Leading up to the trip Felipe had hinted on a few occasions that Brazilian women love American men.

Party's Over

I took it with a grain of salt. My dad used to tell me year after year about the gorgeous woman roaming the beaches of Marco Island, Florida (where my parents owned a January time-share). When I finally made it down there one year, I discovered that, in fact, the beaches were mostly desolate in winter, and the women who were there were senior citizens.

If you're a meat lover, the food in Brazil is to die for. At the top of the list is a cut of beef called *"picanha."* On a geographical map of the cow, it is the rump cap. I've a lot less interest in preparing great food than in eating it; nevertheless, I did take note of some of their methods, such as sprinkling the beef with…rock salt. It just works. And any self-respecting Brazilian restaurant will accompany your selection of beef with scrumptious black beans and rice. Match that plate with a glass of extra-crispy, cold draft beer called "chopp" (pronounced "showp"), and it's go time.

São Paulo has a host of amazing neighborhoods where the nightlife is vibrant, including Itaim Bibi, Morumbi, and Jardins. Loud and crowded, the bars were fun. When Felipe introduced me to a woman, he'd explain that I was visiting from the United States. She'd smile, take another sip of her drink, and go back to talking with her friends. Thank goodness I had low expectations coming in. It wasn't surprising to me anyhow; these were educated women with means and just-fine lives in São Paulo, thank you very much. For what reason would they lose it for an American guy? As I would learn, according to Brazilian women, we're emotionally clogged up, which keeps us from being spontaneous, affectionate, and passionate men. Many believe that the visceral stuff they respond to is largely absent from us.

Chapter 5

MEETING SILVIA

I hadn't forgotten about my pen pal, Silvia. Felipe had been talking to her on and off after I got down there, trying to find an evening and place to meet. They decided on a coffee shop in the center of the Iguatemi Mall. The place was huge, with five levels of stores. The café where we'd meet was in the middle of an expansive corridor. As we approached it, I noticed two adorable little girls racing around a half flight of stairs, going up one set, around a rail, and back down another.

Continuing on, we found Silvia sitting demurely at one of the charmingly tiny circular tables that surrounded the shop. What attracted me to Silvia was simply the great spirit that shone through her photos. Here I was meeting her in person. Silvia had kinky, dirty-blond, curly hair that, she would later reveal, prompted some people to nickname her *Leaosinha*, or "Little Lion." She had big, soft-blue eyes and an upturned nose. We talked for a while, and I thought she seemed a bit self-conscious. It turned out that the girls were hers; perhaps she was concerned that they'd do something embarrassing or that I'd be turned off by the prospect of getting involved.

The gift that was Felipe just kept on giving. He told Silvia that during the upcoming weekend, we'd be going to his parents' beach-front condo at the upscale Riviera de São Lourenco beach and asked her and her girls to join us. She accepted. A few days later, there we were driving east on a Friday evening toward the coast. São Paulo is elevated about a half-mile from sea level, and the descent from the mountains that ring the mainland to the beaches below is spectacular. The condo was inside one of dozens of modestly sized buildings dotting the local road that ran along the coast. The unit had three bedrooms and two baths. As soon as Felipe opened the door, the girls burst in and began exploring. As Felipe showed Silvia and me around, the girls found a hammock slung across the balcony and promptly dove in, pulled it over themselves, and played now-you-see-me. I am happy to report that I had my camera out and managed to capture these photos.

The whole weekend was just what the doctor ordered. The weather in the off-season was brisk but refreshing, the craziness of in-season crowds was nonexistent, and so Silvia and I were able to take several proverbial long walks on the beach. Silvia shared her dream to one day "hide horses on the beach" (remember the *r/h* confusion). She said, "It's just so good to be a leave." I thought about responding, "Silvia, Aleve is a six-hour pain reliever." I swept her up into my arms to carry her across a small stream. Spotting what I was about to step into, she cautioned, "Careful. You are going to fell!"

The ease with which I was embraced by two little ladies and their mom was astonishing. Felipe was a great host, all the way through his dropping me off at the airport for my return flight. It meant a lot that Silvia joined us on the ride back to the airport. The good-bye was a lot more emotional than I'd expected. I was beating down demons and barging through a wall of doubt on my way to launching the billboard and website. There were times that my demons had gotten the better of me. But the genuine interest in me that Felipe, Silvia, and the girls had shown just blew me away.

That weekend began a courtship that would have me visiting again during my five-day Thanksgiving break and again during my Christmas break. I brought work for the weekdays, because Silvia was in no financial position to take time off from work. It is difficult for a woman in the man's world of Brazil. In the United States, we've made a significant amount of progress in putting the sexes on equal footing. But a few of Silvia's bosses were only too happy to use their superior positions to their advantage. They knew she was the sole supporter of two girls. They treated her badly, threatening to fire her if she needed to leave early or stretch out a lunch to run an important errand. Heaven forbid one of her girls fell ill. She would lament, "It is terrible how they explore me!"

During one visit, I'd brought down the textbook for the new college-level corporate-finance course that we were launching at the school. With that, a laptop computer, Word, and Excel, I created a battery of killer lessons that I am using to this day. I also took a daily walk to the nearby Ibirapuera Park, São Paulo's version of Central Park, to get in some in-line skating.

The Billboard

After particularly stressful days at her job, Silvia would come home, exhale, and drop her shoulders. Approaching, she'd plead, "I need a rug." I would respond, "Were you thinking round or rectangular?" She would counter, as she closed the gap between us, "I'm going to quick your ass!"

Life for Silvia was incongruous. She lived in a very spacious, three-bedroom apartment in a building in the heart of the Gardens (Jardins) area. And while she had what I gathered to be a reasonable salary for a professional, money was tight. Looking through the prism of an upper-middle-class upbringing, I couldn't help but feel for her. There was no hot-water service in the apartment. The only water temperatures coming out of the kitchen sink were cold and colder. "How in the world can anyone get grease and oil off cookware and utensils without the help of warm water?" I thought. Apparently, it can be done with a whole lot of dish soap. But the soap was like water; it sucked. The first person who brings Dawn dish soap to Brazil will make a fortune.

The pots, pans, and utensils were a mismatched collection of light-weight stuff. The gas stove and cooktop were so tiny that they looked like something out of a Fisher-Price kitchen. The building had no gas service, but the oven and cooktop used gas. They were supplied by a giant gas tank that took up the entire lower kitchen cabinet beside the oven. Think of a propane tank used for backyard grills, and then think of it on steroids. With no meter on the tank, Silvia would occasionally open the cabinet door and slosh the tank around to assess how much gas was left. The goal, of course, was not to run out of gas halfway through cooking. Not wanting to have this worry during my stay, Silvia proudly announced, "I ordered another tank in advantage of your visit."

Despite the generous size of the apartment, the builders spared no effort in making bathrooms so small they could double as torture chambers. Bathrooms were sit-on-the-toilet-while-brushing-one's-teeth-over-the-sink small, enter-the-shower-enclosure-sideways small, and don't-even-think-about-dropping-the-soap small. It's no wonder why the obesity level is low in Brazil. Once in the shower with a firm grip on the soap, I thought I was ready to go. I had wondered how an apartment with no hot water allowed for a hot shower. I found out by reaching up to adjust the shower head while taking said shower. It turns out that the shower head is electrified, which allows an internal element to heat the passing water. I grabbed not just the head but also the two poorly secured wires sitting on top of it. The result was quite a shock. Water and electricity…I'm fortunate to be able to tell the tale. Had I died, I'm quite sure I would have been found standing up, as there was no room in the stall for a proper collapse.

The toilets were different, too. There was no tank; there was only a button on the wall above the toilet. Perhaps I should have experimented with the button *before* using the toilet, as pressing it caused a rush of water into the bowl. As I soon learned, the water would keep coming until I let go of the button. A second too long meant a rather regrettable splashing on the legs. Thank goodness for small miracles—I initially used the toilet only to do "number one."

There was a small TV in the corner of the living room, an old-school tube with a rabbit-ears antenna that picked up perhaps four channels. It was on that little guy that Silvia later told me she'd caught the tail end of TV Globo's segment on me. The apartment was also devoid of air conditioning and heating. São Paulo is closer to the equator than any part of the United States, which makes it difficult to compare the climate of the Brazilian city to that of an American city. Suffice it to say that it gets really hot in the summer. Silvia's apartment was a corner unit on the ground floor. Her corner sat at the intersection of the major thoroughfare Avenue Nove de Julho (they like to name their roads after dates) and Rua (road) Groenlandia, which passed perhaps twenty feet from her bedroom window. I was stuck between a rock and a hard place: It was either (1) close the window to reduce sound, and lay there melting; or (2) open the window to catch a breeze, but be jarred from slumber by the certainty that the screeches of a truck braking meant that it would be crashing through the wall at any moment.

It's only fitting that each day when Silvia was working I would be served a nice warm lunch with all the fixings by Silvia's…full-time housekeeper. Despite all that I'd accomplished in my life, this was a first. Of course, you are thinking, "How can this woman afford a housekeeper (on top of living in a spacious apartment in a great area of the city)?" It must have something to do with the "favelas," home to Brazil's underclass. We never talked about it, but I am assuming the woman resided in one. I'm not sure Silvia knew, either. The woman was a maid, babysitter, and cook rolled into one. She got there early enough to feed the kids in the morning and walk them to school. During the day, she did laundry, kept the apartment spit-shined, made lunch, and then walked the kids home from school in the afternoon. She stayed with the girls until Silvia returned in the late afternoon. For a single mom, the ability to employ this woman five days a week was a godsend.

In the evenings, we prepared dinner together. Silvia showed me how a small piece of flat metal with a bent corner opened cans. Moving it back and forth, she pointed out how it was working its way around the can. Silvia's eyes met mine as she handed it to me, adding, "See? It's easier than pie."

The public schools that Silvia's girls attended were used for multiple sessions each day. The girls attended the morning shift, from seven thirty to noon. This meant that they'd arrive home with the housekeeper hours before the end of Silvia's workday. With me speaking minimal Portuguese and they (including the housekeeper) speaking no English, communicating was a real challenge. There was a lot of pantomime among us.

Audrey, the older of the girls at the tender age of seven, was very active. She'd practically traverse the perimeter of the living room without touching the ground by jumping from one piece of furniture to the next. When we'd walk through Ibirapuera Park, she'd run ahead to climb some apparatus or another. Within minutes, she'd be staring down at us from a frightening height. Apparently, the Brazilians didn't get the memo about not having anything in the park that could be the source of an injury. Audrey was quite headstrong. When she was upset with her mother, she'd put on a mean face and keep it there. If we were out walking, she'd combine her "bad face" with a stern march that would place her way ahead of us.

The girls were so light that, at some point in my visits, I acquired the habit of tossing them onto their couch from several feet away. They loved to go flying, the farther and higher, the better. If I could cite anything I said that I thought they understood, it'd be, "Don't tell Mom!" When walking about the city, four-year-old Isabelle would hitch a ride on my shoulders. Isabelle's version of "Tom" came out "Tome"—close enough. Isabelle had somewhere picked up at least one word in English: "careful." When I'd have her on my shoulders and begin to cross a street or walk down steps, she'd plead, "Careful, Tome! Careful, Tome!"

With Silvia's apartment being in a vibrant area, we found everything we needed within walking distance. We visited museums and made time for local art fairs and expositions. Exposing her girls to differing cultures and the arts was a high priority for Silvia, as she wanted them early on to have a broad view of the world.

The only dogs Silvia knew were those that her mother kept around the yard when she was growing up. She'd never had a truly domestic "inside" dog, but she decided to get one for the girls. One day when I arrived for a visit, there was a new member of the household named Fadinha (pronounced "Fa-jean-ya"). It was clear that among the books Silvia hadn't read was *How to Raise a Puppy*. For starters, they kept Fadinha in a pantry area behind the kitchen. The two areas were separated by a louvered door and a large window above the sink that was always open. When the girls wanted to play with the puppy they'd bring her into the apartment. When they were done, they'd return Fadinha to the pantry. But they didn't stop talking, laughing, and moving about. The puppy, hearing everything and wanting to be in the middle of the action, would cry—for hours, nonstop. I explained to Silvia that a dog was not a toy that you could put away when you were finished with it. She believed that the animal was fortunate to be safe and have a roof over its head, so my words fell on deaf ears.

Fadinha had no training, so she would not respond to commands. She would also squat anywhere and do her business. OK, that was not a disaster if she went in the tiled kitchen or pantry.

But somewhere along the line, Silvia and the girls realized that if they picked Fadinha up, she wouldn't go. This allowed them to get her out of the building without worrying that she'd go in the hallway. Audrey loved carrying Fadinha. There's nothing wrong with that, but it was how she carried Fadinha that baffled me. Imagine a dog that is standing in front of you and facing the same direction you are. Now, you bend forward and hug the dog behind its front legs. Next, you stand up. You are now holding against your chest and stomach a dog that is facing forward with its four legs flailing about. I hinted earlier that Audrey was quite strong. She enjoyed carrying Fadinha so much that when we'd go outside, she wouldn't put the dog down. Instead she carried Fadinha for blocks and blocks. I am unable to report what the dog was thinking.

Residents started openly complaining about Fadinha. While the pantry faced the interior of the building, its designers had made natural ventilation possible by having all windows on the interior wall of the apartment open to an uninhabited space that was open to the sky above. This ensured a supply of fresh air, not to mention light. It also ensured that Fadinha's incessant wailing would bounce around in an echo chamber and be heard by everybody in the building! One evening we were cleaning dishes in the kitchen when we heard a smacking sound followed by the splashing of water in the pantry. Silvia wondered what it could be. I ventured a guess, "Your neighbors are getting so pissed off that you won't quiet Fadinha, that they're throwing water balloons at us."

One quiet evening Silvia sat me down to explain that she was, in fact, not Silvia Alves, but Sueli Schmitt. Huh? Silvia was her online persona, an identity created to keep strangers and critics and perhaps her ex at bay. Only when she felt she knew a person well enough did she reveal her true identity. And I was just about to get her monogrammed towels.

Over the course of several visits, it was actually the girls who would give the final word as to whether my relationship with Sueli (say "Sue" and then "eh-lee," quickly) would go forward. One of her priorities was to find a man who would be a good father to her girls. If I hadn't given them good vibes, that would have been a deal-breaker. Even though the girls and I could not converse, we got along swimmingly; we made funny faces at each other, played the chase game, and generally acted silly. I passed the test.

Chapter 6

THE CRUCIBLE

The oldest of five children born to Terezinha and Lino Schmitt, Sueli grew up in the small town of Cerquilho, about a two-hour drive from São Paulo. She had a disaster for a father, which meant that she and her siblings were subjected to abuse, neglect, violence, and worse. Dear old Dad did stints away, and all of her siblings, as well as her mom, were deeply affected. Without a reliable breadwinner, the family struggled financially. The number of things this family did without is truly heartbreaking. I won't forget her story about her coloring her sneakers daily to fool her better-off classmates into thinking she had multiple pairs of shoes.

Sueli's thoughts wandered to a life that was better and bigger than the mess that was her family. Her escape came in the form of books. Due to the amount of escaping that she needed to do, she became a voracious reader. At thirteen she took her first job and began contributing her wages to help support the family.

A frequent attendee of Sueli's church was a guy several years her senior. He was educated, well-spoken, well-dressed, and mature. Of course, the bedrock was that they shared the bond of a common faith. What was not to like? At nineteen, she married him.

Over the two years since her high-school graduation, Sueli noticed that her friends had basically disappeared. When she finally asked about their whereabouts, she learned they'd left town for something called "university." Further research at the town library revealed that there was an array of post-high-school educational institutions where people could choose to learn skills to allow them to pursue careers in their fields of interest. She decided that university was for her. She prepared for and took the daunting series of Brazil's uniform entrance exams. They lasted four days. She didn't make the cut at a university in southern Brazil, but she was accepted by a university in São Paulo in her preferred major: fashion. Had she not been notified by a neighbor who saw her name in the announcement section of a São Paulo paper, she would have missed her own acceptance. Her plan was to go to school during the day and work at night to pay the bills. Her husband would hang back to tend to the small bakery they'd opened with some going-away money she'd gotten from her employer of five years. On the weekends she'd rejoin her husband in the kitchen and bake away. When the appointed hour arrived to prepare for freshman year, she hopped a bus for her first trip to the big city. It was one of the few times in her life that she felt completely alone.

Apparently, things weren't complicated enough, so Sueli (unintentionally) became pregnant before freshman year was over. People freaked when she attended classes the next year with a newborn in tow. Her promise was that if the baby became a distraction, she'd leave. The baby obliged. It was difficult to carry a baby along with a stack of books on multiple buses that bridged the distance between her tiny rented bedroom and the university. But the physical toll was arguably the smaller half of it. Her "poor-new-mom" shtick was quite the contrast to the average fashion student in the big city. Her classmates were gorgeous, pampered girls with bounce in their steps that confirmed their lives of privilege. While Sueli fumbled with the bus schedule on Friday afternoons, these girls cackled over whose new Daddy-bought car they would take to what nightclub. She felt alone on Fridays, too.

As we know, Sueli added a second child to the mix three years later. She got her degree all right, but, in order to simulate a supportive family, she had to borrow money to buy dresses for her mother and sisters to wear at her graduation. Later, she hoped to accelerate her budding design career by spending a year in New York City to learn English. By that point, her marriage was irretrievable. And at this point, it would be best that I stop talking about her background. Perhaps if the reception to this book is strong enough, she'll sit down and write her story.

Chapter 7

THE BUILD-UP

Here and there I had been warned that you don't really know people until you spend significant time with them. Those concerned for me just wanted to put it out there. I got their drift. It was a big concern. The largest number of consecutive days Sueli and I had spent together was nine. Anyone can be on his or her best behavior for that long. I had no response. I could stay longer during summer break, but Sueli was unable to take appreciable time off work; it would still not be a close simulation of real life.

Still, I tried to spend as much time with Sueli and the girls as I could. After my initial trip in the summer of 2006, I visited over Thanksgiving. During this visit, I stayed at a hotel. We took a selfie that I carry in my wallet to this day.

The highlight of that visit was a trip to the zoo. By my second visit, we already looked like a family.

Also during that visit I took my favorite photo of Sueli and the girls in front of their apartment.

I visited again just a month later during the Christmas break. Sueli, the girls and I travelled to see Sueli's family in her hometown of Cerquilho.

Audrey and Isabelle with their cousin, Murilo, and dog, Fadinha

Sueli knocking mangos out of the tree behind her mom's house

Sueli's mom, Terezinha, with Isabelle

For New Year's we joined Felipe and his friends and family at their vacation condo. It was a great experience. Felipe, his parents, and his friends could not have been nicer. It is the Brazilian way. They treated us as if we were part of their family.

Felipe and his girlfriend, Sueli and me

Light on the beach was provided by the fireworks.

Sueli's willingness to let it all go and join me in Long Island was evidence of a commitment whose depth was hard to fathom. That she would take this chance on me and entrust her kids and herself to me, meant the world.

The Billboard

Before one visit, I bought a ring. I was so nervous and apprehensive about moving forward that I didn't propose to her until the last day of the trip, right there on the couch. As bold as I'd been in setting out to find a mate was as meek as I'd been in asking for her hand. It was not how I envisioned proposing. She graciously agreed to marry me.

A little research showed that the prescribed way to get Sueli and the girls into the United States was to apply for a fiancée visa. The deal is that once the three arrived in the United States, Sueli and I would have ninety days to marry. Even with the help of an immigration attorney, the process was daunting. This type of visa is rife with abuse; for example, a US citizen charges money (or perhaps not) to marry a person who wants to live in the United States. The couple stays "married" for a few years while the immigrant applies for permanent resident status. Upon receipt, he or she abandons the marriage. Thankfully I had a folder of hundreds of e-mails that we exchanged over the year we dated, phone bills detailing our international calls, and the dozens of photos we'd taken—as a couple and as a family—on our travels in and around São Paulo.

Along the way Congress decided that the Immigration and Naturalization Service (INS) should be self-supporting, and their fees went through the roof. After paying thousands for this and thousands for that, I couldn't imagine how the process could play out for lovers on a budget.

The Build-Up

"Hurry up and wait" was the order of the day. After waiting months and at Sueli's insistence, I started making phone calls to various immigration offices just to make sure they didn't drop our file behind a desk. There was an INS location in Vermont and one in Colorado, I think. We learned that they had scheduled Sueli's hearing months earlier, but had just neglected to let us know. We had thirty days to get a long list of requirements together and be present in Rio one weekday morning at the US embassy. The list of requirements included more proof of the authentic nature of our relationship, medical work-ups for Sueli and the girls, and other personal documentation. Sueli's stomach was tied up in knots as she tried to get all this done while not letting on at her job that there was a good possibility she'd be leaving. My part was easy. All I had to do was fly down to São Paulo, gather up the ladies, and then fly to Rio.

We had found a Rio hotel online that was within walking distance of the embassy. We could not afford to allow traffic jams and accidents to keep us from making our appointment. The hotel itself was an edifice with an art-deco feel and rich wood paneling lining the walls. As is apparently not uncommon in much of the world, the hotel had no air conditioning. And just because one opens the windows, doesn't mean there's going to be a breeze. As we situated our bags, I spied a sizable mosquito dancing in the dim light of a wall sconce. This jogged Sueli's memory. She thought we might want to know that this summer Rio was suffering from what would later be called the 2008 dengue-fever epidemic. "Honey, thanks for sharing," I thought. Down went the window and thus began my mission to locate and eradicate one mosquito. Sueli and the girls seemed less concerned. I didn't know what supergenes they thought they had, but, if it was all the same to them, I preferred to track down the mosquito and eliminate the threat.

During the night, my quest was interrupted by complaints from Isabelle that her stomach was aching. Moments later, the four of us walked out of a perfectly safe hotel at midnight to wander the prostitute-laden streets and alleys in search of a Walgreens. I serpentined down the street to keep the mosquitos from getting a bead on me and rubber-necked for pimps and thugs. Sueli saw me acting strangely and asked, "What the big f is going on?"

Growing up in the white-bread 'burbs, I wouldn't know a gang of real street toughs from a band of emos. By God's grace, we found a store, got what we needed, and made it back unharmed. Lying in bed with the sheet pulled up around my eyes, I ratcheted up my senses in an attempt to see or hear the mosquito, to no avail. I eventually drifted off.

The next morning as the sun came up, I did a quick vital-signs check. My breathing and heart rate were both normal. A quick look in the mirror confirmed that I was not bleeding out of any orifices. All systems seemed to be go. Heck, even if I had been bitten, I figured that the symptoms wouldn't set in until after our appointment. I just didn't want to make a dramatic collapse like Patrick Dempsey in *Outbreak*, or start making awful faces during our appointment as a raging case of diarrhea set in. Immigration agents are the last people you would want to make suspicious.

After waiting in line for the well-protected embassy to open, we made our way inside. When our number was called, we were brought to a private area in front of a thick glass wall. After a few moments, a young examiner emerged from the recesses of the inner office to sit at a desk near the glass. I wondered how cool it was to be an American on assignment with the US government in Rio—not a bad gig for a young person wanting to see the world.

As I observed the setting, my mind wandered to a TV scene of a prison visit. I was just happy to be able finally to support Sueli in a pursuit that had her doing ninety-nine percent of the work. The examiner was courteous enough but so distant, practiced, and robotic that I wondered if the humanoid army had arrived early. At one point in our conversation, I asked for her name. She responded with a pleasant smile but declined to provide it.

We weren't nervous, because we were making a legitimate application that was backed by gobs of evidence and support. But how ill at ease the smugness of these workers makes applicants is truly something to behold. No wonder people around the world think Americans are arrogant.

The Billboard

While in Rio we visited the statue of Jesus Christ
and took in the magnificent views.

Our visa eventually arrived, and we made our plans for
the girls and Sueli to be with me in the summer of 2008.
That would allow the girls to get acclimated before beginning school in the fall. I got Sueli a Portuguese-speaking
attorney to whom I could send a prenup. Sueli made it
abundantly clear that she was not interested in ever assert-
ing a right to any of the assets I'd previously accumulated.
This was a big comfort. She was already making a huge sacrifice, and now this. We got me some life insurance in case
I dropped dead. The whole thing came together quickly. It
had to.

The Build-Up

In the weeks leading up to Sueli's arrival, my preparation went into overdrive. After an exhausting couple of years spent building the dream house, several things were left unfinished. The more time passed, the less motivation I could find to finish them. The two front bedrooms on the second floor shared a spacious Jack-and-Jill bath. Individual vanities sat on either side of a large window. Below the window sat a padded bench. Along the inside of the bathroom were separate enclosures for the toilet and shower stall. I hadn't put light fixtures over the medicine cabinets, on the bathroom ceiling, or in the toilet or bath enclosures. Neither bedroom was painted nor had a light fixture. Wanting to make Sueli feel welcome before arriving, I sent her a layout for the two bedrooms and bath and asked her which room she wanted to give to which girl, as well as what colors they wanted their rooms painted.

With my dad's help, it took a few weeks to get everything completed. Thankfully, he was retired but still quite capable. My other problem was a mountain of stuff that filled one of the garage bays. My best friend Jim had made much of the cabinetry for the house right there in the garage. He had long since finished, but the table surfaces he built and scraps he'd left—not to mention leftovers and unused parts and accessories from the whole project—sat there in a daunting pile. Tearing it all down and trying to find a home for everything took several more days.

The Billboard

Just two days before Sueli's scheduled arrival, we finally saw the light at the end of the tunnel. Dad decided he was going to skip dinner with Mom and that we were finally going to finish bundling up what was left of the garage pile. At approximately 11:30 p.m., while sitting on the floor forcing twine around a bundle of wood scraps, I took a mighty swipe with a utility knife. The knife cut through the twine, continued its downward motion, and proceeded to cut through a good-sized vein in my ankle. I instinctively pulled the knife out and stared at my ankle. My next heartbeat caused a surge of blood to fire out of the cut, through the air, and onto the floor. "Oh my God," I thought. "I'm going to bleed to death before Sueli even gets here!"

I slowly turned and gave Dad an "I may already be dead" look. He rushed over to assess the situation. We got a towel and applied pressure. We elevated the leg. He called Mom. "Sally, Tom just cut his ankle, and I'm gonna take him to the emergency room. I'll call you from there."

Imagining myself as a medical professional, I attempted to apply enough pressure to stop the bleeding but not enough to collapse the vein and cut off circulation to my foot. I hobbled into Dad's car, and off we went. The first emergency room we visited seemed none too impressed. With no apparent bleeding and me not turning gray, I was not the model for which the word "emergency" was fashioned. We waited thirty minutes with no seeming progress for anyone waiting there. We called another ER. Policy prevented the receptionist from indicating their current patient load. She did, however, hint that I might be better served there. So we checked out of the first hospital, I hobbled back into the car, and we drove to the second one. By the time I took my hand off my ankle so the ER doctor could take a look, an hour had passed. The site had already clotted. My foot felt fine. I was going to live! A few stitches later, we were out of there. Dad occasionally ribs me about the look I gave him that night after the first splat.

Sueli's last month in Brazil was a real torment. Closing up her financial affairs there was traumatic enough, but, as the days wound down, she began selling off the contents of her apartment. During the last week, the apartment was becoming so barren that Sueli took the girls to stay with her mother in Cerquilho. One night she called me, crying hysterically, "They took the refrigerator! They took the refrigerator!" The gravity of dismantling everything she'd worked so hard to build had finally hit her. She was sitting alone in an empty apartment.

Chapter 8

THE ARRIVAL

The fateful day was July 15, 2008. I had booked Sueli and the girls on an overnight flight that would arrive in the wee hours of the morning. Mom and Dad were nice enough to accompany me to the airport in their car. We arrived ahead of time. The monitors eventually showed that the plane was approaching, and then it landed. We waited and waited…and waited some more. Then, out from behind the arrival wall appeared a train of carts with bags piled high being shoved from the back by a woman and two girls—bingo! In all, Sueli had brought twelve pieces of luggage representing her thirty-two years.

The Arrival

Finally stateside!

Finally, she was here. She had wanted to make a grander entrance, but was just spent. We gathered that none of them slept much on the way up. That was quite all right. In the parking garage, we piled the bags into Mom and Dad's SUV. When they were loaded up, we made our way to my car. Soon we were strapped in. Just before starting the engine, I took a deep breath. With my woman riding shotgun and the two precious girls in the back, my life had officially changed. I was excited…and scared to death.

The ride home was about forty-five minutes. Occasionally, the girls would excitedly point and shout, "Skeelo!" Sueli translated, "They are excited to see squirrels." The girls rarely saw squirrels where they lived. Nonetheless, they were experts courtesy of having seen *Ice Age* many times.

Mom and Dad arrived at my home earlier than we did. They waited awhile but eventually called to see if everything was OK. They feared that perhaps we had our first fight, and I'd turned around for the airport. It was nothing like that; I explained that I was on the way, but Sueli kept suggesting that it might be a good idea to pull over. About two miles from the house, I did. Carsick Isabelle leaned out the window and barfed down the outside of the door.

Months prior, when discussing her arrival, Sueli hinted that the degree to which she'd feel welcome would be related to the number of people there to receive her. In the condition she was in, she was happy that I'd brought only my parents along. But when we opened the door to the house, the real committee jumped to life and greeted her warmly. Sueli, who felt like crap and thought she looked like crap, was just aghast that this was going to be my family's first impression of her. We should be careful what we ask for.

The girls were relaxed. Before making their way here, Sueli had fed them a little psychological antianxiety medication. She'd told them that they were going to the United States for a two-month vacation. If they liked it, they could stay longer.

An arrival early in summer would give the girls a chance to get acclimated and learn as much English as possible before school resumed after Labor Day. Brazil's location on the other side of the equator meant that we'd pulled them out of their school midyear. We had to decide whether to enroll them in a grade that was either a half-year ahead or a half-year behind where they'd left. With a formidable language barrier, we signed them up to restart the school year they'd been halfway through when they left Brazil.

Prior to Sueli's arrival, I had put up a friend, a retired teacher named Randy, in the far second-floor bedroom. We had him come over each morning for a few hours to teach the girls the basics of English sounds. At six feet five inches tall with a gray beard, Randy was an imposing figure, but he was soft-spoken, empathetic, and not so big when he sat down. In addition, I had bought a pack of index cards to write down the names of objects in the house—faucet, mirror, sink, and so forth—and tape them in place.

Sueli augmented Randy's instruction with drills she'd devised to learn English herself. She'd draw an object for the girls and then write its name in Portuguese. Next, she'd write its name in English. After a bit, she'd erase the Portuguese, leaving only the English name with the drawing. Finally, she'd erase the object and have them redraw it. I have no idea if this is fundamentally sound, but it has just the right amount of nuance to become potentially the next great education method. As the summer progressed, Sueli would exhort, "The quickly you learn English, the better!" God bless her.

Audrey had reached twelve years of age; Isabelle was nine. Audrey had arrived with a few common conceptions about the United States: Everyone is rich, and everywhere is like New York City. These and other conceptions were in need of adjustment. One of the reasons she was excited to come was that she and her sister would not have to attend school. When Randy began teaching them the basics of English at our kitchen table, she adjusted her understanding of the situation: they would be home schooled. Audrey's mind saw the United States populated with rabbits, another animal they didn't see much of Brazil. I asked Sueli why this was so. She replied, "The same reason there are no stray dogs in China...dinner."

The house itself was beautiful but perhaps too big. Sueli got lost a few times. When it was being planned, what looked reasonable on paper wound up much larger in real life. My charge to the architect was to build a place that did the well-situated waterfront property justice. He may have done that a little too well.

The Arrival

There are many benefits to being in the 'burbs. One doesn't have to catch a train to find a green field or a space to play in. And, one of the rights of passage for any self-respecting suburbanite is to learn how to ride a bicycle. It was with great satisfaction that we got the girls bikes and taught them how to ride.

Chapter 9

THE PERFECT STORM

The good news was that I built and completed the house without taking on a mortgage. Still, it was going to be difficult to afford the house comfortably on my teacher's salary. I would need my financial investments, an Internet endeavor, or a spouse to generate the additional income needed for us to truly enjoy the place.

Through the prior half-decade, I had a significant amount of money in aggressive investments. Going into 2007, I believed there was a good chance of a recession, so I closed out my options positions. But as 2007 wore on, the market resumed its upward move, and the news swung back to positive. The stock market (as represented by the S&P 500) rallied through the year and peaked on October 8, 2007, at a value of 1,561.80. This was about ten months before Sueli and the girls' arrival.

The Perfect Storm

When it comes to the financial world, I stay informed. I read and/or scan every bit of news that I can find. It's also my job. Having built a loyal following for my high-school investing course, I'm not about to walk into a class-room and have my students school me about what is going on in the economy or specific companies. Being an avid reader of *BusinessWeek* among other publications, I read carefully the representations of bankers who said that they knew what they were doing with nonconventional mort-gages and in any event had taken sufficient loss reserves to compensate for anything that might go wrong. With *BusinessWeek*'s readership hovering around one million, I could never imagine that the banks could or would mislead or outright lie to an enormous audience about something so important.

As 2007 turned into 2008, the value of my invest-ments was falling precipitously. I was calling my at-torney periodically to give her updated figures for the value of my financial assets, which she'd itemized in the prenup that she was drafting. I'd say "Please lower that number by $100,000." She'd reply, "I did. You called me about it a two weeks ago." I'd say, "That was a different $100,000."

The carnage didn't end, that is, the market did not hit bottom until the S&P 500 fell to 683.38 on March 2, 2009. This 56 percent drop had taken place as if in slow motion over a stretch of 512 days whose ups and downs I felt individually and deeply.

The Billboard

The impact that the crisis and its shockwaves were having on my life hearkened back to other episodes of devastating emotional trauma. But the unfolding crisis served as one never-ending teachable moment in my investing and college corporate-finance courses. Period three at Syosset High School runs from 9:12 a.m. to 9:52 a.m. I can remember one day when the market was going to open significantly down from the prior close. It might have been the day the Congress rejected the $700 billion TARP-bailout proposal. The market opened at 9:30 a.m., right in the middle of the period. On the big screen in the front of the class, I'd set up a list of companies to watch, including several that I owned. When the clock struck 9:30 a.m., stocks began trading and the screen filled with red that might as well have been my blood. As the students and I discussed what was going on, I did a quick analysis in my head. I owned 2,000 shares of this stock and it was down $5. That's a $10,000 loss. I had 2,500 shares of that stock and it was down $3, for another $7,500 loss. I figured my losses were in excess of $40,000 that morning. It was out of control. I was out of control. I was in shock.

Years ago a woman in Texas confronted her cheating husband and his mistress at a hotel. After being escorted out by hotel staff, she waited in her Mercedes for him to exit.[13] When he appeared, she promptly ran him down

---

13 "Trial in Killing of Orthodontist Goes to Jury," *New York Times*, retrieved May 10, 2014.

and over right in the hotel parking lot. That was horrific enough, for sure. But a videotape and witness testimony affirmed that she then drove around and around three more times. I could relate.

In retrospect, I never could have imagined that what was supposed to be a garden-variety recession would turn out to be so deep and severe. It never entered my thoughts that bankers could package and pedal trillions of dollars of toxic mortgage puke around the world or that they'd blow up their own firms just to make a few more bucks.

So, why didn't I ride the market crash all the way out? After all, investments only become losses when they're actually sold. For one, many of my investments were long-term call options that provided as much as two years to work out as I intended. The protracted meltdown proved fatal to them. Another issue was one of honor. Yes, I know it may sound quaint, but, having been burned by what I was coming to view as a thoroughly corrupt cast of characters, I simply wanted nothing to do with them ever again. So at some point I just sold what I owned and walked away.

Against the corrupt Wall Street bankers, the Federal Reserve, compromised credit-rating agencies, finance-channel cheerleaders, clueless politicians, and feckless regulators all selling the prosperity story, I never had a chance. There was actually a name for people in my situation: In Goldman Sachs internal e-mails, employees call the uninformed—the truly misinformed who are led to financial slaughter—"muppets."[14]

And so, with my personal life having taken one giant leap forward but my financial life having taken a giant leap back, I found it impossible to keep one from polluting the other. Yes, I'd made enough money to buy the property, knock down the old house, and build the new house. But any Long Islander will tell you that paying for the house itself is only half the battle. The other half is property taxes (and, to a lesser extent, insurance). The town of Oyster Bay, within which the Big Blue House is situated, was only too happy to have me build it. After it was completed, my annual property taxes were in the low twenty thousands. By the time Sueli arrived, they were about twenty-five thousand per year. A year later, they would be twenty-eight thousand.

A three-headed monster was consuming me. The heads were, in no particular order: (1) a market that I could not count on to earn me anything; 2) the fact that I had gone

---

14 Of course, in the years after the crisis, the market rebounded strongly, easily surpassing 2007's bubble highs. I'm not at all disappointed to be on the sidelines. As I see it, the Fed and other central banks print trillions of dollars to distort markets; companies buy back trillions of dollars of their stock (at all-time highs and with borrowed money, no less) to support their elevated prices; the government publishes specious statistics; the privileged class vacuums up all the wealth; debts are dramatically higher than before the crisis; and banks are more concentrated than before the crisis. All of these lead me to believe the market reflects artificial prosperity. I don't particularly care what level they're at, and I don't waste energy handicapping when the king's horses and king's men will finally run out of the tricks that keep Humpty Dumpty on the wall.

from one to four mouths to feed; and (3) the cratering economy, which meant that, despite her industriousness, Sueli's chances of finding gainful employment were somewhere between zero and none. The life I had worked so hard to provide to Sueli and the girls was no longer tenable. Welcoming Sueli to the Big Blue House on the water with the boat at the ready was a completely hollow experience. Everything would have to go. I was not going to allow myself to become a slave to my possessions. What is more, there would be no maid.

So while I was physically present, arriving home each day sporting the best face I could manage, in every other regard I was far away. Just when Sueli needed a man to be as present, supportive, and intimate as possible, I was nowhere to be found.

Aside from the financial storm, I often found myself a stranger in my own home. As could be expected, in the early going Sueli would regularly converse with the girls in rapid-fire Portuguese. She and the girls would go back and forth. I'd be in earshot feeling inadequate and outside, something I wasn't accustomed to. I only half-jokingly began to wonder if the conversations were going like this:

Audrey: "This guy's a joke."
Isabelle: "I agree. I want to go back to Brazil."
Sueli: "It's unanimous. Let's get out of here."

It didn't help that Sueli carried a huge hole in her heart from her awful family situation. She longed for a father who would step up at crucial times to be her champion. She'd have settled for an uncle or even a big brother. But it never happened. To make matters worse, family members she did try to recruit to help her never spared a discouraging word. "Why do you want to do that?" was the sentiment.

In the more-chauvinistic-than-the-United-States Brazilian culture, it was especially difficult for a young woman to make her way. She was never close with her sisters, but the final insult for them was her leaving the small town. Against this backdrop, I had mentioned that my family was different. My two siblings and I had all gotten postgraduate degrees and achieved our own measures of success. After spending a decade in Atlanta, I chose to return to Long Island, where my brother, sister, parents, aunt, uncle, and cousins lived. We both held out great hope that they would be the family that she didn't have.

As the days slipped into weeks and then months, we tumbled into our first cultural divide. In Brazil when families are close, they see each other several times a week. With my family, it's several times a year. Face time and contact time—physicality—is just not there. "We all have our lives," I'd explain. "There's always something going on. They're there if we really need them." Sueli didn't understand.

We'd walk the neighborhood and admire the beautiful homes, manicured lawns, and planting beds bursting with flowers. It looked like a perfect movie set or, alternately, a postapocalyptic scene where a smart bomb had vaporized the people but left everything else untouched. "Where are the people?" Sueli would ask. "Why aren't the children playing on their big lawns?" she'd wonder. If humans are social animals, then Sueli is superhuman.

Much of Sueli's disappointment was due to a little misunderstanding about what "Long Island" means. In the year she spent stateside in 2004, Sueli had lived and worked in and around Astoria and Long Island City. Astoria is a dense melting pot. Long Island City was experiencing a rebirth, with enormous amounts of money being poured into gleaming new apartment buildings with spectacular views of Manhattan across the East River. Both were a short subway ride to Manhattan. In the years we spent in courtship and planning our lives together, I had mentioned innumerable times that I lived on Long Island. She heard Long Island *City*. I am quite sure I mentioned living an hour outside the city. To her that meant an hour in heavy São Paulo traffic, which equated to a few kilometers of actual distance. But I wasn't that close. Massapequa is thirty-five miles from Penn Station, the heart of midtown Manhattan. Plenty of professionals raising their families in the suburbs hop a one-hour train weekdays to Penn Station and back. They demonstrate every day that it's doable. But when you factor in getting to the Massapequa LIRR (Long Island Rail Road) station before catching the train and then getting to your destination once you arrive at Penn Station, you're up to a one-and-one-half-hour "door to door" commute each way.

Having sat on the tarmac at Guarulhos Airport in São Paulo quite a few times, I know the flight information on the seatback monitor would show a distance to JFK Airport of 4,672 miles. It had to be maddening for Sueli to have come so far and wound up east of her target by a lousy thirty-five miles. Still, I am comfortable that I was forthcoming with exactly where I lived. In fact, it was right there on see-tom.com. The following image proves it!

Sueli's personal frustration was at least offset by the benefit befalling the girls. Long Island's schools are generally excellent, and the 'burbs are a great place to raise a family. Even so, the start of the girls' first school year was rough. Sueli would read from their textbooks every night and translate the content into Portuguese for them. In addition, they were pulled out of class an hour a day for concentrated English language instruction by their ESL (English as a Second Language) teacher.

Thank God they entered our schools in second and fourth grades, where the content and rigor have yet to ratchet up. Audrey and Isabelle's young minds didn't disappoint. I can say without exaggeration that they were fluent in English in six months. Their new hobby was correcting their mom's English: "It's battery, not baytery!" When my family got together a few months after the girls' arrival, they were knocked over as the girls carried on a conversation with them instead of offering only smiles. Not everything was great, though. The girls would complain of merciless teasing by (mostly male) classmates about being from a favela or living naked and swinging from trees in the Amazon jungle.

Save for the encounter Sueli and the girls had with a guy who followed them down the street from a garage sale, our area felt as safe as it appeared. Consider that in nice areas of São Paulo properties are surrounded by ten-foot walls capped by four courses of electrified wires. Here we were in a neighborhood where you could leave a bicycle out in the driveway overnight and no one would take it. A few times over the years I'd been aghast to learn that my garage door was left open all night. Invariably nothing would be missing. It's just a nice place to live.

Having a degree in fashion and another in textiles to go with her decade of experience, Sueli searched for employment in her field. New York City is a major fashion center, so that gave us hope. I can remember many a winter evening working with her to write and refine the ideal cover letter in response to a job advertisement. Not only did she never get an offer for an interview, but she never even got an acknowledgment that anyone received her resume. In 2009, the world was melting down. The pickings were slim, and hiring managers were no doubt swamped with hundreds of resumes. It was not personal. I can remember a job advertisement whose requirements began with a person fluent in Portuguese. It was as if the advertisement was written with Sueli in mind. Surely, if anything was going to come of this heretofore thankless effort, it would be with this position—but no dice. It wasn't lost on me that the ads we painstakingly responded to were likely placed to meet legal requirements, and that jobs were actually going to insiders or persons with connections. Job-hunting felt like a colossal waste of time and, more importantly, of hope.

Sueli was—and still is—nothing if not determined. She turned to internships. Here, she got a different reception. A few fashion houses were happy to benefit from her hard work and experience. She arranged a three-month internship at one company in the city on Mondays, Wednesdays, and Fridays, and a second on Tuesdays and Thursdays.

She was determined to prove her value. On the weekends she'd pore over historical fashion tomes from the local library for inspiration and ideas to bring to the companies. She wasn't overly proud; she embraced the office grunt role to make coffee runs.

The Perfect Storm

A month before the end of the internships, Sueli asked each of the two companies about the likelihood of her internship turning into a full-time position. The supervisor at the company whose business she preferred matter-of-factly explained that not every internship turns into a job, and hers would not. Two weeks later, the intern Sueli had been alternating days with began showing up on Sueli's scheduled days. They wanted Sueli to show her a few things. They got to talking. The girl was young and inexperienced. A drama major, she didn't know how to thread a needle. But she was friends with the supervisor. They even went to yoga classes together. On the first day of the last week of her internship, Sueli went into the office and saw that it had been reorganized to fit an additional desk. When she inquired about it, they told her that the other intern would be joining the company. These a**holes didn't even have the decency to wait a week and let Sueli finish her internship. As I talked with her on her way home, it was obvious that she was crushed. Having always managed to make her own way and figure out how to earn her keep, Sueli took blows like this very hard.[15]

Amid these circumstances we planned and held our wedding. We had no choice; the ninety-day clock was ticking. The wedding was a modest civil ceremony with close friends and family. Most people figured we'd later have a nicer church affair. But Sueli would need to get annulment

---

15 Through LinkedIn Sueli kept tabs on the supervisor at the company. Within a year she was officially "between positions." To the uninitiated, that means she's unemployed.

from her first marriage for that to happen. Due to the attendant complications, the formal wedding never happened. Given the aforementioned financial shell shock, neither did a honeymoon.

Joined by Audrey and Isabelle after we said our vows

My parents have been supportive of us in every way possible!

The Perfect Storm

Things were unfolding so differently than we had imagined. We feared the girls would struggle with a new culture and language and with finding friends in our cliquey schools. But they were doing great. It was Sueli and I, consumed as we were by the Great Recession, who were reeling.

Frustrated, defensive, and withdrawn, Sueli had hours every day after the girls and I left for our respective schools to contemplate whether her leap of faith was an epic mistake. In a feeble attempt to stem the financial tsunami, I had enrolled in several in-service courses after my teaching day to allow me to move up the pay scale. The courses had me coming home much later than normal. Within one year after Sueli and the girls arrived, I had attained forty-five credits. It might be a record, but the pay increase was barely noticeable.

Chapter 10

THE BIG BLUE HOUSE

As depressed as Sueli was, I was no better. Feeling like a failure for selling her a bill of goods she wouldn't be able to keep, it was difficult to come to terms with selling the house my dad, brother, and I had painstakingly designed and saw through to completion over a three-year period.

We had done more than build a house from scratch. We had removed the old one and pulled every bit of its foundation out of the ground. To ensure that the new house would have the most sound footing possible, an excavator had dug down until it removed all organic material (i.e., mud) that could break down and be unstable. From there, we had had to encapsulate tons of crushed gravel until we got to the chosen height of 9.9 feet about street level. We wanted the future home high enough in the air to be protected against damage by any future flood. The completed subfooting work had consumed 250 cubic yards of crushed bluestone.

Starting with a strong foundation by beginning
well below the old foundation

The timeline of the home's construction spanned my return to college to become an educator, a semester as a student teacher, and the start of a new career at my alma mater, Syosset High School. For about a year and a half after returning from Atlanta, I lived in an apartment in Freeport. For the remainder, I lived with my brother Chris and sister-in-law Sue. Squeezing the time frame was Sue's pregnancy. They were running out of room. They'd already moved a crib for their first child into their office to make space. Too many nights, under the cover of darkness, I'd slip into the office to prepare and print lessons. But the zipping back and forth of the printhead made a lot of noise. Each time before I hit that button, I'd cringe. Here and there, the printer noise woke the baby. Lying a few feet behind me, he would prepare to stand up and look around. This was my cue to slip out of the chair and hit the deck. Lying silently on the carpet for as long as it took, I hoped that the lack of anyone to engage him would be the fastest path to him lying back down. More often than not, it worked. Truth be told, for the first year of teaching there wasn't a time when I had lessons completed even a day in advance. I don't recommend it.

My recently retired dad was at the house constantly and willing to do anything necessary to keep the project moving forward. I never would have chosen to act as my own general contractor had it not been for my dad's career in construction.

Trying to do as much of the work as we could, we rented a huge scissor lift that Chris, Dad, and I used to install—over the winter, no less—the fiber-cement siding. The material was so tricky that it took three different saws just to cut a board around a window frame. A small army of Chris's friends and colleagues joined us on the lift for work and for laughs. Dad would cut a board. We'd try to fit it in on the house. It would be a bit too tight. Dad would say, "I'll take off a hair." We'd take the board back down and lay it in front of the saw. Dad would shave its length.

We'd put it back up, but it was still too tight. "Dad," we'd ask. "What did you do, take off half a hair?"

The tricky "around the window frame" siding board.

Months before in my brother's driveway (he lived about a hundred yards away), I had previously laid out the eight-and-one-quarter-inch by twelve-foot siding boards and applied two coats of Cabot's Federal Blue paint. On a good day I could apply two coats to fifty boards. The house was so darn big that over six hundred boards were needed to cover the house. People in the neighborhood driving by would look over at what I was doing. Eventually, they'd stop and ask what I was painting. Motioning in the direction of the property, I'd respond, "For the house across the street." They'd turn to see an empty piece of land.

Before the job was done, everything I wore wound up Federal Blue.

During the three weeks of painting, the house was being built. A company located more than 100 miles away was constructing the floors and walls in panels that would later be trucked down and lifted into place. Our job was to have the foundation, foundation-capping wood sills, and interior piers in place to receive them. Connecting the foundation and the piers were tripled-up fourteen-inch microlams, which are superstrong laminate beams. On the first day I realized that we were going to work with wood, my grizzled construction-veteran dad suggested that I go out and get a tool belt and some tools. The most convenient choice was Home Depot. There I got the essentials, like a hammer, marking pencil, tape measure, and triangular "square." I returned, got out of the car, and strapped on the belt. Dad took one look at my orange belt and plastic square. Unable to contain himself, he shouted, "Hey, it's Bob the Builder!"

The floors and walls were lowered in place.

The standard for supporting a floor is to place beams sixteen inches apart. These floors would have them every twelve inches. The exterior walls were not two inches by four inches, but two inches by six inches. Instead of fiberglass insulation, we had it spray-foamed.

My brother had supervised the rough electrical wiring. We wanted to make sure we planned for everything. We ran a separate circuit to an outlet in the food pantry in case I wanted to add a second fridge in place of the some of the shelving. Ditto for a separate circuit to the master bath in the unlikely case it became desirable to replace the claw-foot tub with a Jacuzzi. To ease the running of the wires in the crawl space, we made a dolly that could roll across the cement floor. I'd lay supine on it and scamper around for hours running wires every which way.

Often when a home air conditioner kicks on, the lights dim momentarily. The air conditioner's compressor is drawing a lot of power when it starts up, and it grabs some from the lights. To avoid these issues, we ran dedicated circuits to the mechanical systems. When the wiring was completed, the house would be served by three hundred amps feeding sixty circuits. If I ever write a book about the building of the Big Blue House, it will be titled, "The Lights Don't Dim at 131 Biltmore."

There were many times when Dad went way beyond the call. In the kitchen I wanted to do a tile configuration called a pinwheel. But I couldn't find a small square tile around which the fourteen-inch, light-gray porcelain tiles would be set. There was, however, a fourteen-inch, dark-blue version of the same porcelain tile that made a great complement. We bought a box of the blue tiles, and, using the tile saw, Dad cut them down to two-inch squares. Next, he used a belt sander to give all four edges a bevel. He worked at this all day so that the tile guy would have the dozens he needed.

The kitchen island sitting on the pinwheeled porcelain
floor that Dad worked so hard to make possible.

In the end, the living space totaled 4,380 square feet.
Radiant heat lay under all of it. The floors were either
quarter-sawn white oak or tile. Ceilings were nine-feet
high on both floors. The house featured forty-five fiberglass windows and forty-five solid wood doors, one-and-
seven-eighths inches thick. There were two wood-burning
fireplaces and two 7.1 surround-sound systems. With the
help of a designer I'd gotten to know well during my stint
in Atlanta, the house, with its mile of moldings, came out
better than I could have hoped. It was both a showplace
and a real home. Its sale would be a loss felt by my whole
family.

It was also difficult to come to terms with selling my dream boat and moving off the water. I am drawn to the water. Boating to me represents freedom, escape, and adventure. The boat I owned, the Tiara 3200 Open, was arguably the nicest thirty-two-footer made. It was pricey but built like a tank and simply stunning. As Chris would always say when he came aboard, "This is not a boat; it's a vessel." Everything on it was oversized, especially the windshield. Hopping up on the helm seat, one's feet no longer reached the floor.

My dreams were crumbling right along with Sueli's. At least it was a blessing to be a teacher. Five times every school day I had to put my issues aside so that I could effectively lead classes. Five times every day I had to unimplode.

Knowing that summer with the boat would be our last hurrah, we took trips to Fire Island and Manhattan. Late in the summer, we decided our last trip would be to Atlantic

City for a long weekend. But come the day of the trip, our issues couldn't be hidden. Sueli was coming to terms with the many ways in which I was not the man she had hoped I was. That's OK. In many ways, she was not the woman I'd hoped for. That our marriage was a trial by fire was never more evident. Did we really ever know each other?

The morning of the trip we walked silently between the house and the boat to ferry stuff we would bring with us. Sueli brought the percolator, not knowing that there was a coffee maker built into the boat. As it was passed between the dock and boat, the lid fell off, hit the water, and was soon out of sight. It seemed only fitting.

From Massapequa, it takes about thirty minutes navigating the Great South Bay to get to the ocean via the Jones Inlet south of Freeport. In silence, we glided over calm seas south and west. Four hours later, after covering about eighty miles of ocean, we pulled into our slip at the Trump Marina.

I'd read that much of Atlantic City was dicey. With two young girls in tow, I had no interest in finding out. We spent the days by the pool and the evenings on the boardwalk. Sueli is not a gambler. If you don't count my participation in the stock market, neither am I. Somehow, we managed to reclaim our spirits. The most memorable part of the trip was recounted by Sueli at the next family gathering:

So we are all walking along the boardwalk. A man in a chairwheel is moving in our direction. He is holding out a can. As he passes close to us Audrey moved in his direction and then returned back to us. A few moments later we heard screaming and yelling behind us. We continued walking because we were sure that it had nothing to do with us. But we heard the yelling and screaming again, stronger and closer. We all turned to see the man in the chairwheel coming right at us. When he got to where we were standing, he waved his can at us. We were so shocked. We had no idea what he was yelling about. Then, he turned his can upside down. A bunch of popcorn fell out. Then we realized that Audrey was trying to help the man by giving him some of her popcorn. We apologized to the man and went back to walking. We all cracked down laughing.

The release of this book coincides with the tenth anniversary of the summer of the billboard. You now know why it took so long to tell the story. I simply didn't have the luxury of time, money, and a decent frame of mind to wax poetic. Further, I had no interest in writing a story that was careening toward a disastrous end. And the time I would need to take away from the family and write the story would have a detrimental effect on Sueli and the girls. I didn't know if the relationship would survive and didn't need to flex the last straw any farther than it already was. At the time, what was keeping us together was simply the decision to stay together one more day. We are a willful pair who don't give up easily. But we all have our limits. On any given day it could have been she or I who threw in the towel.

Chapter 11

You're No Designer

Looking out over the classroom, I'd see boys wearing shirts from popular brands like Abercrombie, Aeropostale, and Hollister. I appreciated their quality, style, and the high-quality "feel" they conveyed. Being a Syosset High School graduate and teacher, I deeply appreciated the value of a Syosset education. Over the years I got the itch to create a classic Syosset-themed shirt of superior quality and thought that the community would embrace it.

Now I finally knew the person who could pull it off: Sueli. She wasn't gainfully employed at the moment. She knew everything about creating garments and had significant Brazilian contacts to boot. Before long we were sitting at a computer wrestling with Adobe Illustrator. Hmmm... How could we bend type along an arc?

We tried to source the shirts locally, but given what we wanted to create, the cost would have been prohibitive. On a trip to Brazil, we hopscotched across sprawling São Paulo visiting all manner of garment makers. Many specialized in one or another aspect of garment production, such as making the patterns and cutting the fabric accordingly, or dying the fabric and washing it (often with a bunch of rocks in the cylinder) to give it the proper texture and finish. Remember the "stone-washed jeans" craze? It's not a gimmick. We found a guy who had a completely nondescript (as in "knock on the door four times, and we'll let you in") but sprawling operation who was capable of doing the whole project.

Normally a big brand will order several hundred samples of a design to send to buyers around the world. If the design is approved, they make several thousand. Our whole order would be a hundred or two. The setup costs in the apparel business are substantial and we weren't ordering enough to really defray the costs. Our guy gave us a great price given the relatively small number of shirts we wanted to order. There was always the possibility of future business if things went well. Really it was because he liked us. He and his "right-hand man" (his wife) invited Sueli and I out to a great churrascaria in town where we had an epic meal.

Perhaps a little too much wine made its way to our heads. When all was said and done, we had committed to producing three Syosset-themed designs and one Long Island–themed design. Sueli and the girls planned to spend much of the following summer in Brazil. She would work out the details, like sizing, and the girls would stay with their father. From New York, I would create a brand and logo, incorporate the business, establish a web page, and otherwise get ready to sell Syosset shirts like none other.

The shirts themselves were the nicest thing to come out of this endeavor. Between the time that we had done some back-of-the-envelope math and the time to send money to Brazil for payment of the shirts, the US dollar had dropped against the Brazilian real. This raised the cost of making the shirts. The cost of shipping came in higher than expected, as did the tariff. So much for free trade.

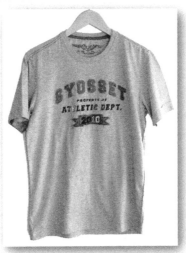

After the shirts arrived in late summer, I got in touch with the presidents of the PTAs of the various schools in the district. There are seven elementary schools, two middle schools, and one high school in the district. I concentrated on the elementary and middle schools, trading messages with many of the moms. I eventually reached them all. The typical conversation:

> Me: My wife and I have produced three super-quality Syosset-themed shirts that you can sell to parents to raise funds.

> PTA President: Oh, we've had such a bad experience with our shirt suppliers. They make us order in advance, and sometimes we don't sell as many as we thought we would. We wind up losing money and are stuck with a bunch of shirts nobody wants.

> Me: The good news is that we've already produced a batch of the shirts. You would buy from us only what parents buy from you. That way you won't be stuck with any.

> PTA President: One year, instead of making the shirts in advance, we

took orders. But our vendor took so long to make them, the parents lost interest. Plus, it was hard to get the shirts into their hands once we received them.

Me:

I have a solution for you. At the next Parent Open House, we will supply you with an ample number of each size and style. You lay them out on the table. The parent grabs the one she wants and pays you for it. After the event is over, you pay us for the ones you've sold and give us back the unsold shirts. Sound good?

PTA President:

We always have problems with our shirt vendors.

I was absolutely sure I had entered a twilight zone. How often does someone, when offered a perfect solution, insist on thwarting it? Person after person was unable to understand. I don't think they had ulterior motives. It just didn't register with them. The reaction was the same, call after call. At the end of the day, I got a positive reception from one of the seven elementary PTA moms. She sold dozens of our extra-small and small shirts. All parties walked away happy. What happened in the two middle schools? One was already set to sell a shirt commemorating the school's fiftieth anniversary, and it didn't want competition. The other said the principal thought a table in the hall during the open house would make the halls impassable.

Something else I had not considered is that Syosset's high-school students, the very boys I'd envisioned wearing the shirts, are "too cool for school." While in the midst of it, they could not appreciate the quality of a Syosset education. Or, they simply didn't care. Perhaps school pride was too "eighties" or "nineties." At a High School event where the shirts were being sold, a parent would pause at the table, pulling her son over while brushing a shirt and taking in its softness. She'd ask if he wanted one. He'd shake his head. She'd ask again. He'd shake his head again. She'd shrug. They'd move on. At this point it is appropriate for you to conclude that the shirts were a significant money loser.

Sueli and I had come at this effort from completely different perspectives. As with the billboard and website, I thoroughly enjoyed the creative process. I am still jazzed and proud to have created these shirts. For whatever reason, and despite my not being nearly as flush as I used to be, the loss just didn't bother me.

But Sueli was downright pissed. What a waste of a summer, of money, and of energy for her. She spent a summer running around São Paulo getting them made and stressing over each detail. She sweated out the transit of the shirts from Brazil to the United States and the escalating costs. It was one thing not to make money. It was entirely another thing to invest on so many levels, receive such an indifferent reception, and lose money. She was not involved in the project for recreation, and this episode stuck in her craw. If you ever meet Sueli, please, I beg you, don't ask her about the shirts.

Is there a bright side to this endeavor? As a family, we have a significant supply of casual shirts. The Long Island shirt is my favorite. Its beautiful navy blue (with deep-red thread) looks great with tan, gray, or plaid shorts. The image of Long Island is comprised of thousands of embroidered stitches. We've even got Shelter Island and Gardiners Island in there. I'm wearing one as I write this. If you were to scan the family's summer-photo albums, it would not be unreasonable to conclude that I own just one shirt.

Chapter 12

IT'S A MAD, MAD WORLD

There are a few themes running through my relationship with Sueli that I just have to look at with levity. My "Frontgate meets Pottery Barn" standards were going bye-bye with the meltdown. Meanwhile, Sueli and the girls brought with them a different approach to living.

We have many lights in our house, especially in and around the kitchen. There's a row of seven halogen bulbs recessed into the ceiling, two incandescent bulbs in fixtures over the kitchen island, and then another row of seven halogens between the island and the appliances. As well, there's a path of halogens leading from the kitchen, around the corner, and into the entrance hall. Halogen bulbs provide a beautiful lighting effect. They also cost a lot, throw off a ton of heat, and burn a lot of energy for the amount of light they provide.

The Billboard

I've had meetings with Sueli and the girls about our wasteful ways. Attempting to get some buy-in, I suggest to them that perhaps if we just left the two conventional lights on over the kitchen island we could signal that someone's home and save energy at the same time. We gather around the bank of light switches. We all know which one controls the two over-counter lights. We agree that when we go to bed, it should be the only switch that is turned on. As fate would have it, I'm usually the first to come downstairs each morning. This allows me to observe a lighting configuration that may change day to day but which, most importantly, is never just the two over-counter bulbs.

The girls have been teased at school about their Brazilian origins and all the stereotypes that come with it. But there is at least a kernel of truth to some stereotypes. One such truth is that Brazil is hot, and Brazilians are accustomed to that temperature level. São Paulo is in the southern half of the country and feels like it's about midcontinent. But it is actually closer to the equator than Key West, Florida. There is a lot more to a locale's weather than just distance from the equator (elevation, for example), but here it serves as a sufficient entree to the point that Sueli and the girls like it hot. I grew up understanding that the human organism was generally comfortable at seventy-two degrees Fahrenheit. It is said that if people move from, say, New York to Florida, over the years their blood will thin out. As a result, a temperature that used to feel comfortable will feel chilly. Perhaps normal room temperature for these folks will be a few degrees warmer than seventy-two.

Sueli and the girls arrived in July to perfectly suitable weather. Eventually though, summer leads to fall and then winter. The change is gradual enough to take in and prepare for. The first winter the girls got all excited to see snow for the first time. They jumped around the backyard grabbing at it like they were…kids.

But inside the house, their goal was to approximate a tropical clime to the greatest extent possible. This meant taking showers so long and so hot as to peel the paint off the walls. When Audrey walked around in short shorts and a spaghetti string top one too many times in the middle of February, I realized that something was up. I don't visit her room often because it's a little out of the way, but it was time. Stepping through her bedroom doorway was a revelation. The twenty feet of baseboard radiator was hot. For added measure, Audrey had commandeered an electric heating tower from the attic and had it blowing full blast.

Audrey uses her room's boxy thermostat as a makeshift hook over which she hangs one of her small canvas paintings. I carefully lifted the painting up and away to assess the damage; it showed eighty-six degrees. I went ballistic; Sueli urged restraint. We'd had this discussion before, several times. So there I was arguing with a teenager over why I'm not going to allow her to keep her room any temperature she wants. What's money to a person who never earned any? I slid into a "save energy, and save the planet" spiel. We are, after all, raising a generation of tree huggers, no? Long story short, there are only three months of "balanced" natural gas bills waiting for me at the low rate of $456 per month.

Toward the end of any given school year, the atmosphere becomes strained. The teachers grow tired of (some of) their students, and vice versa. Instances of bad behavior are inversely related to the number of days left in the school year. For the last few years, come June I've found myself especially wiped out. Sometimes after I return home and greet the missus and the kids, I wander around the house in a discomforting daze. Other times I will find an armchair in the family room to disappear into. In no time I'm off to la-la land. When I come to, I'm in a delirium. I begin hearing sounds…the tapping of a keyboard…people talking to one another. It's as if I am coming out of general anesthesia. It takes several minutes to open my eyes. It's unlike me. Rousing slowly, I try to figure out why. Happening by the first-floor thermostat one day, I got my answer. It was eighty-two degrees in the house. The lovely Sueli had gotten into the habit of turning off the air conditioning, allowing the sun to penetrate the windows, and turning the place into a greenhouse. Seeing that I was about to protest, Sueli shut me down before I could get a word out, saying, "Save energy, save the planet!"

Sueli hasn't taken to aging very well. One day she sat the girls down for a serious conversation. "Girls, Thomas and I are not going to live forever. I'm in my forties now." In unison the girls interrupted, "Mom, you're 37!" Sueli replied, "I am almost there. I feel like I am going down to the hill."

We love our coffee, the stronger the better. Powder-ground Brazilian coffee makes Starbucks seem like muddy water. You can cut it with 50 percent milk, and it's still dark. We usually buy the Pilao brand, preparing it by pouring boiling water through a finely screened, coffee-filled cone. It drips through to a tall metal thermos. I set up the thermos just beside the cooktop and near the wall. This way I'm not swinging a kettle of boiling water around and there's less risk of someone knocking the contraption over.

Sueli prefers to set hers up on the kitchen island. That's fair enough, since we don't have young kids around. Making coffee is not a messy affair, but it's not always pristine. There's a loose funnel between the cone and the thermos. If we can't wait, we'll often pour a cup's worth while the cone is filled and dripping. If we're not paying attention, we'll make more than the capacity of the thermos and the excess will drip over. The counter is dark-colored granite that we've never been able to stain. And so I can't help but wonder why Sueli begins her coffee setup by placing a clean yellow dish towel on the counter! On it goes the thermos and coffee-filled cone. If the idea is to stain a towel, well then, she's almost there. Come to think of it, she's never been fond of yellow.

Food in general has been a big area of contention. I've learned over the years how to play—and mostly win—the game.

The Billboard

There's a difference between "cheese" and "cheese product," as well as between "juice" and "juice drink." Despite the drumbeat of conventional nutritional wisdom, I've been served well by eating proteins and fats while avoiding carbohydrates.

I don't help Sueli with food preparation as much as I should. Sometimes she'll prepare the ingredients for a meal and then turn it over to me. Motioning toward the pan, she'll instruct, "Put this to burn."

I'll never forget what went down the very first day after Sueli arrived. She poured the girls glasses of orange juice. They sampled it and apparently pronounced it "no good." After a brief conference, Sueli went to a cabinet and returned with the sugar bowl. She heaped two spoons into each girl's glass and stirred. They found it much better.

The other natural resource they have an appreciation for is salt. More than a few times I've been in the kitchen talking to Sueli as she prepared meat with vegetables in a pan. I've watched the big Morton salt container be taken out of the cabinet and waved back and forth over the pan. The more the white crystals rained down, the greater the horror that came over me. Sueli would notice and protest "You're taking the joy out of food!" Actually, I was just trying to avoid a heart attack.

Food isn't always contentious. We both like a great salad. To get one started, Sueli usually pulls out leafy greens, dried cranberries, sliced almonds, and some feta cheese. I take it from there. Midway through she'll suggest, "Honey, you can even add some chicken peas."

I've always made sure that nothing sits on the stairs. That's just inviting trouble, which I've been living with ever since Sueli arrived. You name it, I've found it at the top, the bottom, or somewhere in the middle of the stairs: Dryer balls? Yes, balls in general. Pillowcases on their way to the laundry? Of course. Flattened boxes? Check. Hats? A good fit. Shoes? Absolutely. Magazines? Affirmative. Towels? Please. Vacuum attachments? The vacuum hose? Area rugs? All of the above.

There have been times when Sueli is in some clean-up mode where she so fills the landing with garbage or laundry that the area is simply unpassable. If I'm not up for adventure, I just walk out of the house and try to get to my destination by entering through another door.[16]

In case life isn't surrendering its share of humor, I get to participate in the inadvertent practical joke. Reaching for the granola box to grab a bar on my way out the door, I find myself lifting an empty box. It seems that the person who took the last one never learned that the appropriate thing to do is to throw the box away. This doesn't just apply to boxes. I've found empty bags of apples, juice-box packages, printer-paper wrappers, and even the occasional empty half-gallon of milk. Good thing I wasn't looking forward to that scrumptious Saturday morning cereal with bananas!

---

16 On the day that I wrote this chapter, I returned home to find that the lovely Sueli had emptied our pantry onto several stair treads, essentially giving every cereal box, can of tuna, and bag of rice stadium seating.

The Billboard

The beginning was almost imperceptible: a simple super-market bag hanging on a doorknob. She'd done this in Brazil, but unlike in her apartment I had ample receptacles for the kinds of things that she regularly placed in the bags. They're called garbage pails! I'd remind her, to an indifferent shrug. Sometime later, another bag appeared, and then another. I now deal with garbage in small units, like rabbit droppings.

How do you clean a spot on a tile floor? I used to apply a simple spritz of a mild cleaner and wipe it up with a paper towel. But with Sueli's help, I realized that I'd been doing it wrong the whole time. The correct way is to commandeer a bucket, fill it with lots of hot water and soap, soak an ample supply of rags, and then scrub the spot and a wide area around it.

Invariably, something would grab Sueli's attention before she could clean up after the clean-up. Or, maybe it's that the batch of soapy water she whipped up was so effective, she wanted to keep it at the ready for the next spill. The result is a bucket of dirty water in the laundry room. Wait; was that a second one in the garage? Could there be a third in the downstairs bathroom? If Sueli cannot locate an empty bucket, she'll scrounge for any that she could find. It does not matter if the chosen bucket has tools or gardening implements in it. Those must be displaced as collateral damage in the war on dirt. A bucket must be filled, and it must be filled now.

Our marriage has brought a new appreciation for life's simple luxuries. Take, for example, bedsheets. I used to change them out as a set. But one sheet suffered a rip, the other was stained, and a pillowcase went missing. Tonight I will lie down on a green fitted sheet, a light-blue twin-sized flat sheet that doesn't quite cover the queen mattress, and a pillow in a beige case. It is possible that a flat sheet might be substituted for a fitted one. I hadn't previously considered that bedding could be so eclectic.

Being an expert in clothing and textiles, Sueli takes great care of her clothes. She hand-washes many garments and chooses to let them drip dry. That's all good. It's not so much the hanging of the clothes but where they are hung that impresses me. If it'll hold a hanger, it's fair game. After pulling the car into the garage nowadays, I have to run a gauntlet, because my wife has recently discovered the overhead garage-door tracks.

Over the years, I've accumulated an array of household cleaners. Not every product is suitable for every purpose. In my house, if it has a sprayer top and it's nearby, it's the right product. "Honey, that's Windex. It has ammonia. You shouldn't use it on the stainless steel." "Honey, that's furniture polish. The kitchen-cabinet finish is sealed. The polish won't absorb." "Honey, that cleaner has acids in it. It's not meant for the car." Oh, never mind.

The Billboard

At 3,500 square feet, our current home is big. It's just the four of us, so we have plenty of room. But Sueli's favorite household accessory has become the over-the-door rack. We've got 'em not just for closet doors but for bedroom doors that have no hidden side. Granted, they are a godsend for city dwellers trying to make a go of it in tiny apartments. But a rack will often slide back and forth on a door, scratching it. Its brackets scuff the door frame when the door is shut. A rack will clank each time its door is opened and closed, and its presence invites random crap to be hung from it. Right now there's a giant paella pan on a hook just inside our coat closet. That bastard really makes a racket.

I was raised to view the wasting of food as a sin, because so many people in the world go without. But it happens. There have been times that Sueli has made a wonderful batch of potato salad for this party or that barbecue. The event gets cancelled and, the next thing we know, we've got several pounds of potato salad going bad. What should we do? Return it to nature, I've learned, is the answer. On garbage nights, said potato salad was one of several food items I'd notice go missing. It was no longer in the refrigerator, and I couldn't find it in the garbage pail. It seemed to have vanished. Months later, while raking the planting beds I'd find a mound of indeterminate origin. Ah, there's the potato salad! It's nice to achieve closure.

It's a Mad, Mad World

On any given day, I'm likely to find labels left on cookware and glassware that are in use, salt in the pepper shaker, garbage placed at the curb any day of week, items placed face up in the dish rack, dish towels used as shower mats, dirt swept into a pile and then left in place. I tried to resist. Really, I did. I protested. I fought. I got loud. I went quiet. Eventually there was resignation and then acceptance. My journey into the unknown continues.

Chapter 13

STRAIGHT TO YOU FROM NEW YORK CITY, NEW YORK!

With the reception, or lack thereof, that Sueli got from corporate America, I increasingly encouraged her to do her own thing. Given the time involved in and the cost of commuting to Manhattan, unless she got a high-paying job, she'd basically be working for nothing. I also knew that the recession had ushered in an era of many more people wanting jobs than there would be jobs. Employers would gain the upper hand, and Sueli and most other employees would be disposable.

Sueli hatched the idea of creating a Portuguese-language blog about fashion and travel in New York City. We tossed around ideas and looked for available Internet domain names. With the World Wide Web already ten years old, the pickings were slim. We settled on the name FashionSpill, registered the domain, and began the trademarking process. Our next step would have to do with selecting the platform on which the site could be built.

Thanks to the power of the free markets and the open-source movement, several content-management systems (CMSs) exist that allow individuals to create attractive websites at very little cost and with no coding skill required. The CMS Sueli selected was Wordpress. She chose a look for the site by selecting from among several dozen templates that govern the color, layout, background, and general appearance of the content, like magic. Having worked in software development before becoming an educator, I appreciated only too well that the cost of developing the capabilities offered by this platform from scratch would be prohibitive.

Soon Sueli was writing articles not only about fashion and tourism, but also about Americana. She tooled away day and night on her laptop, doing extensive research in her quest to write definitive content.

One day Sueli was preparing an article on American movie icons from the fifties. She was looking for the name of a young man she described as being the epitome of cool, who always seemed to be walking down a city street while taking a drag of a cigarette. He had tragically died in a car accident after having made only a few movies. She inquired, "Was it John Deere?"

As her base of articles grew, she began appearing at the top of Google's search results. To monetize her growing awareness among Brazil's tourists, she became certified as an NYC tour guide and then began offering tours. Sueli is fascinated by the role that New York City has played in the development of America. She is equally captivated by—to cite the History Channel series—*The Men Who Built America.* On a road trip to Florida that consumed twenty hours of driving each way, her companion was T. J. Stiles's 736-page tome, *The First Tycoon: The Epic Life of Cornelius Vanderbilt.*

Every now and then while reading, Sueli would learn something so notable that she just had to share it. The girls and I would be deep in conversation. Sueli, announcing her intention to interrupt us, would say, "Sorry to cut you."

It was great to share our love of history. Together we watched all seven parts of PBS's *New York: A Documentary Film,* a history of New York City. We visited the Museum of the City of New York for its exhibition of the audacious plan from 1811 to ensure that north of 14th Street, Manhattan's thoroughfares would follow a uniform grid. It was prepared without regard to topography, and it called for massive changes. Hills would have to be leveled and creeks filled in. Each north-south avenue would be one hundred feet wide. While the land making up the future avenues and 155 cross-streets would be leveled, not so the surrounding land.[17] After the roadways were leveled, it was not unusual for a home situated beside an avenue to

---

17 Wikipedia.com, "Commissioners' Plan of 1811."

find itself on a precipice several floors high. The maps and surveys on display at the museum showed the future road system overlaid on existing private farms, structures, and other features of the land. It didn't matter; the grid was coming through. Can you imagine trying something like this today?

We extended our interest in New York City to movies set in New York. One we've seen together is *The Gangs of New York*. Sueli was heard to inquire about another, more famous movie: "Honey, this weekend can we watch *The Goodfather*?"

I am going to venture a guess that Sueli knows more about New York City than the vast majority of New Yorkers. Its history is just fascinating. For example, in the 1600s a barrier was erected across the lower portion of Manhattan to keep the Dutch settlers in the south separate from the native Indians to the north. It stretched from shore to shore, blocking a prominent Indian trail. The barrier was, of course, a wall; it was located on what is now Wall Street. We know the trail as Broadway.

Today, the worldly Sueli offers tours of Central Park, Wall Street, Brooklyn, Soho, and Tribeca. She's even added a tour of Long Island's North Fork wineries. For those who share her love of history, she offers a mansion tour. Because of her background she's also a great resource for all things fashion. Future brides have enlisted her assistance in finding the perfect wedding dress. Owners of retail stores in Brazil have sought her help in navigating the wholesale scene for new goods. The best gig so far has been providing the occasional single woman a guided tour of—and some company at—the city's rooftop bars.

In the summer I will often go into the city in time to meet up with Sueli after a tour. We'll visit some hot spot like Bryant Park or the Meatpacking District. Feeling the energy of the crowd (along with the alcohol in a single glass of wine), Sueli will confide, "I don't know why I'm married. I like to flitter!"

While the meltdown was disastrous on many levels, I made tough choices to ensure that it didn't completely wreck us. We're in a financial position where Sueli can be selective. I try to get her to appreciate the fact that her not having to chase every dollar or accept any offer is a blessing. She is truly her own boss. Most significantly, she's decided to do small-group tours only. They consist of a family or a few couples and are much more personal; there are no buses or cattle calls or counting off to deal with. In their place are opportunities to linger as well as photo ops galore. Strangers at the start of a tour are friends by the tour's end. Sueli's extensive knowledge, combined with her vibrant personality, can make one's visit to New York City truly special. I am very proud of her and the career she's made for herself.

Of course, it always looks like roses from the outside: nothing but laughs with clients while spilling out of one luxury store and into another. But there have been more than a few hiccups along the way. To differentiate her site,

Sueli wanted to add an area that provided translations for fashion terms between English and Portuguese. She envisioned providing a picture or illustration with each term. Because Sueli is often asked random questions by people who find her site, also she conceived of a front-page window within which people could pose questions that other visitors could answer. It would show the history of questions asked and answered. Thankfully, Wordpress allows for such custom extensions and add-ons to be added to a site, but you've still got to identify a software developer who can bring them to fruition. One thing led to another, and, before I knew it, she was Skyping with a developer in India. Shortly thereafter the guy had developed these features as well as a completely customized template. Now FashionSpill.com looked exactly as she wanted.

This was all cool until one day she called me in a panic. "The site is down. Please, try to access the site. I think it's down!" Sure enough, it was down. We scrambled and called the company that hosted the site. Turns out they were not happy with one of the extensions installed on the site. It was running inefficiently and hogging way too much in the way of computing resources. They didn't know which extension was causing the trouble, so they just turned the whole site off.

The hosting company shut down FashionSpill so quickly because the site was one of several running off the same server, an arrangement that's known as shared hosting. Anything that clogged her site also affected the other sites. One option suggested to Sueli was to upgrade her site to dedicated hosting. This would have her site, and only her site, running on a server. Upon learning of the enormous price differential, she proclaimed, "What a hip off!"

There were hours of back and forth between the developer and the hosting company. Stress is the responsibility for an outcome (i.e., the site being brought back live again) without having the ability to affect that outcome (i.e., neither of us being programmers). By this time, Sueli had built up site visitorship to more than one thousand per day. Friends and customers would contact her to let her know the site was down. "Yes, we know." We'd uninstall this and roll back the other thing. She'd stay up all night poring over HTML code. She knew that every hour the site was down meant dozens of potential followers and future customers who might never return. I'm not even sure what the resolution was. On account of the stress, I may have blocked it out. All I know is that we eventually got the site back up and running.

We were now fully dependent on a smart, well-meaning guy in India. Every now and then, we had minor outages. Most of the time he'd be responsive. But who knows what was going on in his professional life or personal life? The idea that her whole online brand depended on one person half a world away was just nuts, in my opinion. When Sueli was out of town I dedicated a day to carefully poring over hundreds of commercially available Wordpress templates in search of one that would most closely meet Sueli's needs.

She had to get away from the custom template we'd allowed her to become a prisoner of, even if it meant doing away with a custom feature or two. Thankfully, I found one that made her content look clean and orderly. But it still provided for the ability to highlight articles and videos. Scrolling down the site, visitors could browse articles by topic. Visiting the demo site, I captured and printed each screen section. Stitching the sheets together using scotch tape, the sample was several feet long. It was instrumental in making my pitch. Sueli liked the look and agreed that it was time to get off the roller coaster.

By this time Sueli had authored over one thousand articles. Each had at least a few pictures. While this would necessarily consume a substantial amount of storage space, for some reason her site's files were just enormous. For a reasonable fee, the company behind the chosen template proposed to export all of her content out of the Wordpress database and then to import it into a new database. It worked! The space her content consumed shrank by ninety percent. The site was now much faster and more reliable. Using my intermediate Photoshop skills, I created a new banner for FashionSpill that launched with the new template. It was a whole new look that her readers received warmly.

Over time I basically became the in-house IT department. Sueli would wear out a laptop computer within a year. Sometimes a key would pop off and disappear. Sometimes she'd choke the hard drive with so many photos that the thing would slow to a crawl. Shaking her head in front of a nonresponsive PC, she once suggested, "Maybe my computer was racked."

Sueli was truly a pioneer in bringing valuable travel information to Brazilians who intended to visit New York City. But there were "low barriers to entry," capitalism-speak for "it would easy for others to do what she does." And so it began. A section of Sueli's site was called "Dicas de Nova York," or "Tips for New York." Someone created a website using this as a domain name. But one would think that surely a base of one thousand articles would allow FashionSpill to remain the definitive travel resource for New York City–bound Brazilians. Yes, it would have, if the purveyor of the new site (among others) had any integrity. Instead, to populate his site, the guy re-created Sueli's most popular articles. Imagine reading an article and simply rewriting it in your own words. It would take but a few minutes. Do this for a few dozen articles over a day or two. Congratulations, you're in business! The copycat slipped up with one of his articles and basically lifted one of Sueli's word for word. We produced a side-by-side comparison for his site's hosting company, proving the blatant ripoff. They took his site down for twenty-four hours, explaining to us that this would give them time to contact their client and for him to "correct his error." Gee, thanks.

On the challenges of being the boss of a business and its only employee, Sueli declared, "My stress affects my mood and my appetizer."

What began as a trickle became a deluge. Brazilian celebrities living in New York City began blogging about living there. Popular Brazilian magazines offered special inserts containing everything a traveler needed to know about New York City. Even New York City got into the act by translating various tourism materials into Portuguese. Sueli's lead in the marketplace had not led to critical mass. Instead of riding the wave of Brazil's broad discovery of New York City, Sueli was drowning in it. Pushing back was painful, frustrating and a colossal waste of energy.[18]

Besides, the influence of these competitors paled in comparison to the real power, the true kingmaker: Google. In February of 2011 it introduced Panda, code name for a new algorithm it would use to rank search results. If a Brazilian Googled the Portuguese equivalent of "travel to New York City," FashionSpill.com was among the first couple of results, and rightfully so. But Google was bothered by the high rankings of opportunistic sites that quickly write and post articles on currently hot topics. Using Panda, Google "shuffled the deck." According to Wikipedia, "The change aimed to lower the rank of 'low-quality sites' or 'thin sites,' and return higher-quality sites near the top of the search results."

Regardless of the motive, FashionSpill.com was caught up in Panda's net. It was really painful to see a website that

---

18 When Sueli began her site, she intended to devote it equally to fashion and to tourism. Over time, it has found the most traction when its content is about tourism. Now that the site almost exclusively serves tourists, we rue the day we chose the name FashionSpill!

copied Sueli's article on tips for traveling to New York City in the winter (many Brazilians don't even own a winter jacket) ranked pages ahead of her own article. After all, the copied article is newer, and so it would seem "better." Thus began the "Panda period." This "Dark Age" is characterized by a woman reading complaint after lengthy complaint and commiserating with owners of other sites and businesses that were devastated by Panda. It is marked by a woman carefully poring over Google's twenty-three-point vague and absurd blog post on what counts as a quality site. It can be depicted by the image of a woman spending days and nights rewriting and updating definitive articles in an attempt to reclaim her site's prior status.

Alexa.com is the go-to resource for statistics on website visitorship. One evening during the "Dark Age," Sueli logged into the site to check FashionSpill's recent figures. It confirmed that the fall in monthly hits had continued unabated. Unable to contain her anger toward Google, she yelled, "Those f**king mothers!"

A cynic might opine that Google rewrote its algorithms to ensure that formerly high-ranking sites would be severely demoted and would have to pay Google to regain their prior ranking. Founded in the shadows of dominant Microsoft, Google's motto is, or perhaps was, "Don't Be Evil." So the cynic's explanation couldn't possibly be correct. In the end, there was no recovering from Panda. FashionSpill.com had become just another of the great unwashed, one of dozens of sites competing for the attention of future travelers to New York City.

One would have to be naïve, however, to think that anything could keep Sueli down. All the tours she has done over the years, all the goodwill she has created, all the care she gave, provided referral and repeat clients.

Still, the blows kept coming. Supported by China's booming growth and seemingly insatiable demand for all manner of natural resources, Brazil experienced an economic surge that had its Real currency achieving an exchange rate of 1.70 with the US dollar. But the Chinese miracle ended, the air came out of the Brazilian economy, and the exchange rate raced to as high as 3.40. Intrepid Brazilians who shrug off a struggling economy to plan a trip to the United States are nevertheless punched in the gut with the reality that their contemplated American vacation is now twice as expensive as it was five years ago. Not surprisingly, many are staying home. And so we go back to the drawing board.

Chapter 14

BATTEN DOWN THE HATCHES

Wen we moved out of the Big Blue House, we decided to stay in the same school district for the kids. The girls had quickly digested English and were performing above grade level. They were our brightest spot. So down the block we went, buying a corner home off the water less than a mile away. I chose it for the better neighborhood and for the beautiful beach club. The kitchen was new and high-end. Because the economy was still in the tank and other parts of the house were in poor condition, we were able to get it for a good price.

Our new home, which sits on a corner property, was the opposite of everything I find attractive. It had been added onto at least twice, which gave it a slightly Frankensteinian vibe. With low ceilings and every room seemingly on its own level, its bones were awful. The exterior was even worse. The pink siding mimicked rough-cut cedar shakes. But it had discolored badly over the decades. Large swaths had turned completely black. There was a driveway leading up to the house, but the garage had been converted to living space. Usually when a person looks at a home, the front door anchors the appearance. The front door of this house wasn't in the front. It was on the side and not visible to anyone looking at the front of the house.

Before we began packing up at the Big Blue House, Sueli insisted on our making a video in which I walked through the house talking about various decisions that'd been made which resulted in it looking as it did. It was the last of our memories. When we finished filming, she announced that it was time to pack. It was a month before our move-out date. I thought we had plenty of time to pack deliberately. She was right. We scrambled to get out of there on time.

Poor Sueli swallowed hard and didn't say a word about my choosing an awful house. She dutifully toiled away to make the move as smooth as possible. All the while, one question ate at her: Did hers and the girls' very presence prompt Tom to decide to sell his beloved home? Despite my assurances that I, and I alone, was responsible for the circumstances leading to the sale, Sueli remained unconvinced and guilt-ridden.

The home we were moving into was set up as a mother-daughter (i.e., a home plus an apartment for an immediate family member). Behind the former street-level garage was a second kitchen and a bathroom. A flight of stairs off that kitchen led to two bedrooms, one over said kitchen and one over the former garage. The apartment could be accessed from outside via a back sliding door that opened into the kitchen.

Over the first winter, we decided to convert the enclosed living space back to the two-car garage it had formerly been. We did not need the apartment and we preferred to find homes for our cars. With somewhat tough winters, having garaged cars meant not having to step into freezing vehicles every winter morning. It meant not having to scrape ice and snow off the windshields. It meant that the vehicles would not bake in the sun all summer. It is amazing to see home after home with two-car garages that have vehicles worth a total of $100,000 parked out front in the driveway. Perhaps the cars are leased; many people turn their cars in after three years, so they just don't care about treating them well.

The house was full of surprises. Below the five tall windows that had been installed across the space formerly taken up by the garage doors was a newish poured foundation. In front of the foundation was the home's natural gas and electrical service. At substantial additional expense, the foundation would have to be removed and the services rerouted. I had renovated a house during a prior life in Atlanta. I'd built another. Before buying this house I somehow couldn't figure out that a highly unusual twelve-inch-deep front wall (think foot-deep windowsills) would hold some surprises. That major error added thousands to the cost of converting the space.

Letting nothing go to waste, Sueli suggested that we take the tall windows and install them along the back wall of the family room. We did it and light poured in. "Good call, honey," I told her.

The landscaping around the house contributed to the home's sorry impression. At the side of the driveway in an area bordering a neighbor's property was a parched rock garden and two old, scraggly, dying cherry trees. They were something out of a horror flick. The proper procedure was to apply to the town for permission to remove them. Perhaps they'd say OK but only if I planted four trees else-where on the property. Perhaps they'd just say no. There are some times when "a man's gotta do what a man's gotta do," so I lined up a tree guy and had the trees cut down.

I went to work that day wondering if busybodies were going to capture cell-phone video out their bay windows that would be instrumental in convicting me for crimes against nature. Unbeknown to me, Sueli walked outside to chat with the tree guy while he was doing his thing. She instructed him cut the less-decrepid of the two trees back, but not down. She tried to contact me at the time, but I was in the classroom. Eventually we talked, but the tree guy was gone by then. Sueli described what she had instructed the guy to do. I had no idea what she was talking about, but when I arrived home, I found a "superstump" about a foot and one-half wide by eight feet tall. This beacon sat just three feet from the street. I was aghast. I wondered if I should grab a chainsaw and quickly carve it into a totem pole or perhaps a bear. My adjoining neighbor freaked out. Marching out of his house upon seeing me, he barked, "Thomas, what the hell is this? That tree is on my property!" Oops. "If a town guy drives by he's going to fine me, not you, for cutting it down!" Double oops. I apologized profusely and pledged to take responsibility for the fallout. Mostly, though, I blamed it on my crazy Brazilian wife. Being married himself, his tone immediately softened. We commiserated. The tree guy came back the next day and finished the job.

The next winter we decided to bite off something bigger and correct the most serious flaws in the house's exterior. We moved the front door to the front and created an attractive new approach with columns supporting a portico. We also had the house newly sided with a neutral-colored cedar-shake-style vinyl. The renovation was a hit throughout the neighborhood. Finally, someone had done something about that eyesore! "The house looks so nice," a friend of Isabelle said to her (translation: "We felt so sorry for you."). Another compliment came from a friend who called and asked with a hint of distress where he'd gone wrong in trying to reach our house. Through my kitchen window, I could see him sitting in his car at the curb. He was at the house; he just didn't recognize it. It came as a tremendous comfort that my wife said, while we were checking out the landscaping one day, that the house looked beautiful now. We had spent a reasonable $75,000 and gotten back our self-respect.

But not long after, the house tripped on its Achilles heel. In late August of 2011, we watched a developing storm in the South Atlantic with interest. It's rare for a tropical storm to make it all the way to New York with any strength. Those that do visit the area usually move offshore and then harmlessly dissipate. But the prognosticators were making a lot of noise about this storm. It was big, strong, and likely to still have juice by the time it reached us. I got busy preparing to keep the water out of the ground level of the house. In the front, that meant laying and securing a heavy plastic sheet up against the garage. In the back, it meant caulking the sliding door shut.

Not having a mortgage on the house meant not having to purchase flood insurance. The FEMA flood program had a bad reputation, anyway. The deductible was high. Homeowners would be compensated for flood damage up to the point at which walls could be painted, I'd heard. A little self-insurance seemed like the thing to do. But as the storm took shape, I began to feel like a stupid ass for the double sins of buying a home with a low elevation and then not insuring it for flooding.

Contributing to storm preparation, Sueli suggested, "Why don't you go right now to the ATM and download some money?"

What a God-awful feeling it was to be a sitting duck, watching nervously as the experts reported the storm's likely track. The house couldn't be moved or raised. It was too late for flood insurance. I was a stuck pig. Irene (were you thinking Sandy?) didn't disappoint. The water first appeared in the street hours before the brunt of the storm was scheduled to hit. It began coming up out of the storm drains that connect to the canal just one house over. Water slowly filled the street and then began working its way up the driveway. At some point the storm surge crested the canal itself and began pouring into the back yard. Sueli grabbed her camera and went into photojournalist mode. All of her Facebook friends got the lowdown in real time. She filmed our kayak floating by the back window across what was the lawn.

When water reached the house, it began seeping in around the garage doors. When it hit the back door, it worked its way under the door and the frame itself. There was no stopping it or denying it. In a while the water level inside reached about an inch and a half. This was the height of the cement lip that fronted the entrance to the crawl space. At that point the water began pouring into the crawl space, which was about one thousand square feet and eighteen inches lower than the level of the ground floor. Not until it those eighteen inches were filled would the water level on the ground floor rise above an inch and a half. Slowing the water's intrusion dramatically slowed the rate at which the crawl space was filling.

Having done what we could, when the rain stopped and with the tide peaking, Sueli and I ventured outside, down the driveway, and into the street. Standing in knee-to thigh-high water, we met up with neighbors. Finally, something got them out of their homes. A neighbor's boys took turns in their kayak, paddling up and down the street. For a while I again had waterfront property. Like a seasoned storm watcher, Sueli kept her camera rolling. We lingered. The late-summer water was actually quite nice.

Nature's power is just stunning. Anyone who has spent a significant amount of time boating, fishing, or diving respects the water. A gallon of water weighs over eight pounds. A cubic foot of water weighs over sixty-two pounds. The equivalent weights of air are not so much; water is hundreds of times denser than air. You feel tremendous resistance when you are in a pool waving your arms back and forth in the water but not when you wave your arms through air. The point is that air appears to be a "joke" compared to water. But there we were, staring at millions of cubic feet of water happily sitting in places where gravity and sea levels usually prevent it from appearing. Why was that? It was due to air—moving air, to be more precise. The continuous winds over several days had pushed along a massive amount of seawater. When the storm made landfall, so did the seawater.

While making small talk, everyone kept watch for the water level to crest, at which point we would retreat to our homes and prepare to unbutton. At the storm's peak, water was nine inches above our home's ground level. The garage doors held against the pressure. The sliding glass door in back was the bigger concern. For a while there, its glass made the outside floodwater look like one big aquarium. Thankfully, the glass did not give way.

Before the storm began its retreat, it had filled the crawl space with a foot of water. I asked Sueli to be ready to help dry the floors. She wanted to drive to lower lying neighborhoods. Never mind that the one car we'd left at the house would have begun floating, had she backed it into the street. I pleaded with her to help and offered that she could drive around later. This totally defeated her purpose, which was to see the havoc the storm was wreaking at its peak. She thought that she might never see something like this again, and she was pissed. To me, it seemed surreal to go to marital war at a time like that.

When the water receded away from the house I peeled back the plastic and threw open the garage doors. Cutting the caulk allowed the back sliding door to be opened. Warm August air flowed through the ground level. A helpful neighbor came over with a gasoline-operated pump that made quick work of the water that had accumulated in the crawl space. Mops and squeegees gathered up the water that remained. Bing, bang, boom—within two hours the place was basically dry. It was a miracle ending to what could have been a debacle. My fear turned to confidence; I declared, "If that's what it takes to survive a twenty-five-year storm, we've got it made!" Flood insurance? We don't need no stinking flood insurance! We did have it made, all right, for…oh…about fourteen months.

Batten Down the Hatches

Our beautiful kitchen is about five feet above our ground floor and perhaps another foot higher than street level. A step down from the back of the kitchen is the expansive dining room. Beyond the dining room and another step down is the sunroom. To the left of the dining room at the same level as the sunroom is the enormous family room. The steps up and down should be a nuisance, but after a while we barely notice. They make for a more intimate "sunken" family room.

The fall of 2012 was shaping up to be an ordinary autumn, with landscaping begging and Halloween on the mind. On a weather channel one evening, we noted some talk about Mother Nature sneaking in a storm that would probably amount to nothing before the door closed on hurricane season. Without the warm summer water to feed on, the storm was likely to fade. But over the ensuing days, the coverage of the storm became more prevalent and more serious in tone. The storm was to remain intense all the way through its impact with the New York City area. We were just a few days away from potential disaster. Once again I was visited by the ghost of sitting duck. The self-flogging would have reached a fever pitch except that there was work that needed to be done.

We had done some rudimentary planning, like gathering flashlights and making sure there was food and water around. But I had to think about our vehicles, which would all surely flood if this storm was even a shadow of what forecasters were predicting. We had to find places for all of our belongings that were at ground level. During our time in the house, especially given two renovations, the downstairs kitchen, with its large open area, had become a dumping ground. There was a reclaimed, shallow pine chest there, because we couldn't find a place for it. It had so perfectly anchored the upstairs foyer in the Big Blue House. A beautiful green love seat that had adorned the blue house's living room met the same fate. My ice-hockey equipment was there, as were small appliances like a clothing steamer. There were also lots of boxes we hadn't opened since the move. We had to find better positions for our stuff, even if it just meant placing them on the thirty-six-inch-high countertops. Irene had brought nine inches of water. Even if Sandy added another foot or two of water, those items would be OK. It was harder to find high elevations for bigger items like the snowblower that sat in the garage. For this storm I did away with the plastic and simply direct-sealed the garage door to the ground with silicon. I sealed the sides and the joints up several feet. Then I sealed the sliding door again with silicon and this time barricaded it with plywood.

On the morning of October 29, 2012, during the high-tide cycle before the storm was to arrive, Sueli and I began moving our vehicles north about a half mile to a church parking lot that bordered Merrick Road. As if to preview what was in store, this high tide had brought a significant amount of water to the streets. In order to get back home after dropping off our last vehicle, I had brought along a bicycle to ride back home. The rain and wind were becoming more intense, portions of the street were flooding heavily, and the ride was eerie. The immediate difference between Irene and this storm was the temperature. The air was chilly and the seawater chillier.

We'd made the decision to stay in the house and bear the storm. The highest point to which we could retreat was the master bedroom, a good fifteen feet above street level. There was simply no way the water was going to reach that high. Earlier there was some discussion about getting the girls out of there, but they wanted to stay with us. Storm-reporter Sueli never doubted for a moment that she would stay. Apparently she has a passion for witnessing epic events.

In the middle of the afternoon the power went out. We understood this to be a preemptive move by the power company to avoid the chance of electrical fires starting due to eventual floodwaters reaching electric panels in homes. At that point the most notable stimulus was the ominous roar of the wind through stiff, shriveled fall leaves. The only thing left to do was wait.

As luck would have it, Sandy's landfall was supposed to coincide with high tide, which would give floodwaters a boost of several feet. In addition, there would be a full moon, the lunar phase that is most influential on the tide. We were in for a veritable triple-whammy. We wandered around the kitchen, dining room, and family room, periodically checking the water level in front and back. Just a few hours before the peak storm surge, all was quiet.

Perhaps, we hoped and prayed, we were going to dodge a bullet.

It was not to be. A few minutes later Sueli sounded the alarm. Peering out a window in the back of the family room, she announced that the lawn three feet below was now under water. The water level was rising—and fast.

Then we suddenly heard the sound of a large amount of pouring water. We opened the door off the main kitchen and listened down the half-flight of stairs to the ground level. The garage and sliding doors in the back were doing their job of retarding the entry of storm water. Where could water be pouring in from? There could only be one place. The water had reached the level of the crawl space vents, those large rectangular holes in the side of the cement foundation. Whereas Irene's waters didn't reach that height and could not fill the crawl space via this direct route, Sandy would have it filled in a few minutes.

We shut the door to the stairs and ground level, as if that was going to accomplish something. Just a few minutes later, the anxious silence was broken by a loud bang coming from the downstairs. We reopened the door and took a few steps down. Water was now rushing in around the door leading to the garage. The water pressure must have blown out one of the garage doors and was now trying to blow out the inside door. The ground level began filling up like somebody drawing a bath.

From the other side of the first floor, Sueli announced, "I think she's going to come into the family room." We'd previously shoved the dining-room table up against a wall to make space for the family room's couches. That lifted them a step. But other items, like the contents of bookshelves and our small electronics cabinet, were still in the family room. The scramble began. Sueli and I grabbed the TV and moved it into the dining room. We then grabbed the electronics cabinet, its contents, and items from the lower levels of the bookshelves, and dumped them on the couches in the dining room. Sueli was right. The storm was coming for the family room, and flood the room it did. After the crawl space filled, the water just burbled up through the spaces between the slats of the subfloor and then the planks of the oak floor. The sunroom, at the same level as the family room, suffered the same fate.

The water was also working its way up the half-flight of stairs that leads to the lower kitchen and garage. There were only six steps. The storm had already made it up three.

Sueli opened the front door and stepped out onto the covered platform. I joined her as she filmed. The house now was completely surrounded by water. One of the roads that our house sits on does a little zig zag at the corner. To keep delinquents from cutting the corner by driving across our lawn, the prior owner had installed several large volcanic rocks along the property line. Such rocks trap a large amount of air when they are formed, which makes them relatively lightweight for their size. "There!" Sueli shouted over the storm. I followed her outstretched arm and finger to several objects floating by. "Our rocks. They are like turtles."

There are many stages of damage a home can sustain. The most severe, of course, is the stage in which the home caves in and is actually destroyed. Slightly less severe-looking is when the house is lifted off its foundation and sent floating, even if only a little. The house might look salvageable, but it is almost assuredly destined for demolition. At the midpoint of stages on the damage scale is the home whose kitchen has been flooded. The electronics in the appliances will be shot. Steel will begin rusting. Cabinets and door faces will warp. Trapped water behind the cabinets will spawn mold. Floors will buckle. Electrical wires running to appliances and outlets will have to be replaced. In fact, the whole kitchen will have to be ripped out. But if you're one of tens of thousands whose kitchens simultaneously go bye-bye, good luck getting your kitchen replaced. Think for a moment about how a kitchen supports modern living. Its refrigerator keeps perishable food edible. Its cooktop and oven allow for the preparation of that food. The cooktop can even act as a makeshift heater. Its sink allows for food and nonfood items alike to be cleaned. Its table and chairs allow a family the ritual of eating a meal together. A home that has lost its kitchen is dramatically worse off than one that has not.

It was in and around this time that we began "kitchen watch." Just another sixteen inches or so of water and our beautiful, functional kitchen would be toast. We were still well more than an hour away from when the storm surge and tide were projected to be their highest. We spent most of our time upstairs, going back down to check on the water level when we mustered the courage. Against the darkness and pounding rain on the windowpane, we noticed a faint orange glow in the distance. We later learned it was a home going up in flames. A generator had been supplying power to the home, and something obviously had gone wrong. Some part of the flaming home blew to the adjoining home and set it ablaze. I wondered, "How the heck can two homes burn to the ground in a hurricane and flood?" As unlikely as it might seem, it was happening.

Looking out the front of the house, we heard the alarms of a neighbor's two white Mercedes vehicles. The lights on the cars were flashing as well. Then, we observed them begin to float away. They didn't get far, coming to rest at the foot of the driveway.

Using a bedroom that adjoined the apartment via a second door, we accessed the back stairs to the lower kitchen. Walking down partway and casting our flashlight beam down, we witnessed a pool several feet deep with the fridge floating face down in the middle of the room. The same had occurred to the reclaimed chest and everything else we hadn't elevated sufficiently.

The thought of wading in and scooping up what I could crossed my mind, but I was just too spaced out. "We did what we could, and we'll live with the fallout. I am not going to play Aquaman right now," I thought to myself.

The water was unstoppable. Soon it was two steps from the kitchen; then it was just one. The water had begun to bubble up through floorboards in the dining room. Another room was lost. We had raised our couches to that room for a margin of safety, but Sandy just would not relent. The water level reached the couch skirts and began soaking the fabric. Moments before we had scrambled to get the TV and electronics cabinet to higher ground still, which meant finding room for them in the overcrowded kitchen.

It was still a solid hour before high tide and just a matter of time before the kitchen would fall. Then, something happened: Coming back downstairs several minutes after my last observation, I took a good hard look at the water level on the stairs. It had stabilized. There was a lot of water in the house, but it was not rising. Another check a few minutes later confirmed that the water had not claimed any more ground. Then it dawned on me. This bastard of a storm had pushed millions of gallons of water onto land to a depth of several feet. The water is not supposed to be there. It requires an unbelievable amount of continuing force to keep it in place. The force of all that flood water wanting to move its way back into the ocean had finally matched the force of the storm wind trying to push yet more water onto the land. High tide be damned. The storm had finally become a victim of its own success. The stalemate continued for a while. But eventually, the force of the storm abated, and the water began beating a hasty retreat. Within two hours it was gone from the house. The four of us hit the bed. It was a little easier to lay my head on the pillow knowing the kitchen had been spared.

The memories of that first day post-Sandy are a little hazy. The first thing we noticed in our once-over around the house was that the lower half of one of the garage doors was turned inward. Its side wheels were still sitting in the track that was blown off the wood frame and twisted like a roller coaster. Of course, the sliding door in the back—the *glass* sliding door—was totally unscathed.

A line of pine needles and debris stuck to the exterior of the house at the high-water mark. The height was forty-six inches above ground level. All the belongings we'd placed on the lower kitchen's thirty-six-inch-tall countertops were ruined. At least it wasn't close.

The mechanical systems fared poorly. The boiler, situated in the crawl space, was completely swamped. The bottom two inches of the electrical panel was flooded. The water reached just high enough to pour into the outer sleeves of all the wires heading down and out of the panel. Sandy had accomplished a trifecta; we would have no heat, no hot water, and no electricity any time soon.

We walked to the church parking lot to assess our vehicles. They had suffered no damage. We started one up and drove around looking for something warm to eat and drink. In the next town over and just north of us, we found an open 7-Eleven. There was an eerie quiet in the store, because everyone was in shock. Back home we met up with other homeowners and learned of each other's damage. Jimmy, our stoutest, handiest neighbor looked like he'd seen a ghost. He was the guy who lent me the sump pump that emptied our crawl space after Irene. So handy was Jimmy that he'd turned his downstairs rooms into cherished recreation space. The rooms flooded almost to the top. He was shocked to the core but able to muster one suggestion: Order a Dumpster now. We did, and it was placed in the driveway by the afternoon. The south shore of Long Island may have been immobilized, but at least business was taking place elsewhere.

Mold can start growing on soaked organic surfaces very quickly, so it was paramount that we start cutting away and removing soaked Sheetrock and insulation. Basically we had to start tearing apart our house.

We swung open the heavy steel door on the short end of the Dumpster and began to walk pieces of our house into its far end. To make the eventual reconstruction as expedient as possible, we cut the Sheetrock with a utility knife to a height of just over forty-eight inches above the ground. That's the width of a board of Sheetrock. The stuff was wet, flimsy, and heavy. Because the storm hit so late in the season, it was also cold. Wet and cold do not make for a good combination. We mindlessly beat a path back and forth all day.

During one of our walks out to the Dumpster, Sueli and I witnessed a well-dressed young lady having a leisurely walk with her dog. She must have descended from one of the few homes whose elevation allowed it to avoid flooding. We paused for a moment and watched as Fido sniffed around the growing mountains of street-side debris, confident that it never crossed her mind to offer help to any of the distressed homeowners she passed. Amazed at the scene, Sueli turned to me and asked, "How bolivious can people be?"

There are many ways to downsize. This is a new one: Have your stuff ruined and then throw it away. There was a vacuum, the aforementioned clothes steamer, an iron, several circular saws, drills, tools, rollerblades, toys, furnishings, and appliances. If it was wet, it had to go.

In the afternoon we went out and found an open Dunkin' Donuts. The line there was one hundred feet long, and the cold wind made it seem much longer. Back at the house, two neighborhood kids came by and helped out. Boys, if you are reading this, please come by for a commendation letter.

A few friends stopped by to pitch in as well. That night we tried sleeping in front of the gas fireplace. Its incapacity to throw off enough heat to offset the cold was laughable. We ventured back upstairs and did our best to stay warm under several layers of blankets.

Word of our plight had spread through the Brazilian underground. (Wonder how that happened.) By Saturday a small army of women arrived by train and car to clean what they could. It wasn't difficult to keep them busy. There were muddy floors and water stains on things we wanted to salvage. My sister Joann and brother-in-law Michael came ready to put in a full day of work. We needed it.

By far the worst part of the ripping-out had to be the waterlogged fiberglass insulation in the joists under the main living spaces. Most of it was so waterlogged that it fell to the floor of the crawl space. But many sections were held in place by copper piping running just below the joists. Anyone who tried to grab the insulation and tear it down would suffer a stream of cold water running down his or her arm. A sponge pales in comparison to fiberglass insulation in terms of ability to hold water. We came up with a method of removing it. We drag sopping clumps of insulation into a two-person sled, drag the sled to the entrance to the crawl space, lift it up and out, drag it to the Dumpster, lift it over a side wall, turn it over, and let the insulation fall out.

Jim and his wife Lori in Bayside offered to put us up for a few nights. It was our first chance to get hot showers. We packed the kids and started on our way. But we had an issue with fuel. The last thing we needed was to run out of gas in the middle of nowhere, so we detoured for gas, which was easier said than done. Our power company, LIPA, was woefully ill-prepared for an emergency. For a week or more, there was no power throughout much of Long Island. Many gas stations had fuel in their underground tanks but no power to pump it. With each closed station we passed, our fuel level fell and our stress level rose. Eventually we found an open station. Situated on a corner, it had a line of cars leading down one street and a second line down the cross street. It was a return to the gas shortage of the seventies.

Having established my position in line, I got out of the car and did some recon. Instead of capping people out at a certain number of gallons, the station owner was filling people's tanks to the brim and only accepting cash as payment. There was bound to be a lot of disappointment in that line, as a result. Eventually our car inched its way onto the property. We were almost there, and tension was peaking. An attendant assured me that they had plenty of gas left. Minutes later as we were being gassed up, the word went out that they were officially out of gas. Ours was the last vehicle to get it. We made it to Jim and Lori's, where they treated us to amazing food and sleeping accommodations.

We spent another weekend at my parents' home in Huntington on Long Island's north shore. They were already snowbirding in Florida when Sandy hit, so we had the run of their house.

One day a tricked-out camper arrived in the next-door neighbor's driveway. No, his old college buddy from the Carolinas had not just shown up for a visit. The neighbor had rented it as temporary housing. With big disposable income come big options. Not being too proud or too flush, I did the next best thing and ordered a trailer.

A few days in, the Dumpster was loaded to the gills. I called the company to have it taken away, and the driver, when he arrived, backed his flatbed underneath it. The hydraulics groaned mightily in their quest to get the thing aboard. Later that day the trailer replaced the Dumpster in the driveway. The ability to stay on our property was a big deal as school would resume sometime soon and the buses would make their early morning rounds through the neighborhood.

We ate out a lot after Sandy. Sueli would typically suggest, "Honey, let's go to Friday's or Huby Tuesday."

A half hour west, in Long Beach, sewage treatment plants had overflowed and caused a real sanitary problem. They had no running water, and the area was quarantined for a while. At least our toilets continued to work. We had running, albeit freezing, water, as well as natural gas. We had access to our house. Our clothes were safe and sound. It was disaster junior. Still, for spoiled folk, it was a lot.

Three inches of snow came down the first evening we had the trailer. As we lay in the forward bunk, the propane heat was going full blast. But Sueli and I just couldn't get warm. The coldest part of the space seemed to be the bed itself. We took to moving blankets from over us to under us. It was a sleepless, miserable night. The next day I peeked around the trailer's far side, which was visually blocked by shrubs. The door to the two-foot-by-two-foot storage compartment was propped wide open, by whom we'll never know. The compartment ran all the way across the trailer and directly under the bed. The storm had been blowing its cold air in there all night.

Batten Down the Hatches

With the jarring experience that was Sandy, one begins looking around for what else might go wrong. With my forties about to give way to fifties, Sueli came to grips with the difficulty she would have supporting herself and the girls in my absence. She asked, "Honey, do we have enough life insurance in case you pass out?"

God bless Chris Barrella, my one and only brother. He sprang into action almost immediately after the storm hit to get us back into our home. Acting quickly, he asked a friend in Connecticut to visit an HVAC distributor and drop $2,500 on a wall-mounted "instant-hot-water" boiler. All the boilers in the area had been spoken for, and with each passing minute, it was less and less likely that one could be secured anywhere at any cost. Unlike me, over the years that he'd renovated a home or two, Chris had acquired an understanding of plumbing and electricity and the skills necessary to work with both. After several weeks of fits and starts, he got the boiler installed and connected to the heating and hot-water piping. We alternated the plumbing work with pulling and replacing every electrical wire that had been compromised. He installed a new electrical panel and connected the new wires. Everything checked out. All systems were go.[19] Long story short, we were able to move back into the house in a month. All things considered, it was amazing. Being able to sleep in our own beds again was a pleasure. Taking hot showers was even better.

---

19 Both the heating and electrical systems have been redone by professionals.

It would have been nice to relax, but significant problems remained. There were two large framed openings between the kitchen and the dining room. Through the dining room, we accessed the family room and sunroom. We had to gut all three and stack their contents in other areas of the house. I placed a bed quilt over each of the two doorways and encouraged the family to pretend these rooms didn't exist. We took the same approach with the downstairs. It wasn't essential living space, so we tried our best to ignore it.

But poor Sueli, who was working from home in an environment that was upside down. We had heat, but we did not have insulation in the crawl space. It was critical that the area be dry and free of mold, so the insulation would have to wait. But without it, the heating system couldn't keep up, and, on really cold days, the house was chilly. We resorted to electrical heating towers that produced a comforting column of warm air. I'd come home after working to see Sueli in a heavy coat sitting with her laptop at the kitchen table. A nearby heater would be blasting her lower half. Upon seeing me, she'd flash a "How much longer?" look. She had to tough it out until winter turned into spring.

The following summer we put the downstairs back together, sans the lower kitchen. A major shout-out goes to a great friend and business associate named Magno. He sent over a small army of tradesmen to put the house back together. New metal studs were installed. The existing wood studs that we couldn't change out were sealed. Our new insulation was waterproof foam board. The new wallboard was waterproof Durock. We were hoping never to have to tear the place up again. Thanks to Magno and his workers, by midsummer we were able to walk around the house without thinking of the storm.

It's said that no good deed goes unpunished. In contrast, in this case, no amount of personal irresponsibility was punished. Not having insurance meant that we qualified for FEMA aid. Because the extent of the damage was beyond the maximum amount available from FEMA, New York State and the Red Cross provided additional assistance. Because the house wasn't completely wrecked and I was able to get rebuilding assistance from many great people, the flood wasn't a major financial bath.

It may even get better. In the aftermath of the storm, word spread of the creation of a FEMA-funded program called New York Rising. My neighbor suggested that I go into the local FEMA office and put in an application. I did, and months later the office sent an inspector. A few months after that, we received notice that we would be granted a significant sum to raise the house. Wow! The grant is pro-rated over three years, meaning that if we leave the house within that time period, we have to pay back a portion of the grant to the program. The architect told us that we would be out of the house three to four months, during which time we would get a new foundation. We scrambled to get it done during the summer of 2015 but were unsucessful. If things go according to plan, our home will be lifted during the summer of 2016. The saga continues.

We wondered how the Big Blue House fared in the flood. We heard through the grapevine that the floating dock broke loose and floated to the other side of the canal, and that the water made it up to the first floor but did not go in. I still haven't talked directly with the new owners about Sandy. They knew that we bought a home in a hole, and it would be too awkward for them to reciprocate with a question about how we fared.

Chapter 15

LIVING IN AMERICA

Sueli periodically asks the girls if they'd like to move back to Brazil. Besides the fact that they have formed some nice friendships and are not eager for another upheaval, their answer is, "No. We're Americanized now." Let's see: iPhones? Check. Starbucks? Check. Laptops? Check. Musical instruments? Check. Dance lessons? Check. Bicycles, skateboards, and rollerblades? Check.

Sueli, on the other hand, is, um, Sueli. She's a tough nut to crack. Following is a typical conversation between us, one which took place soon after she and the girls arrived:

"I've signed up Audrey for recreational soccer," I said.

"How often will she play?" she asked.

"I know she'll have a game each Saturday or Sunday afternoon," I generalized. "Isabelle is asking if she can play a sport."

"So, if one has a game on Saturday and one on Sunday, that will completely blow up our weekend. We won't be able to go to the city or anywhere else we want to spend the day?"

"Basically," I offered, adding "You are also expected to stand on the sidelines the entire game, rain or shine. We don't want the girls thinking we don't care!"

"I don't understand your country. In Brazil the kids have to occupy themselves. Here it is as if the parents exist to serve the children," she said.

"You figured it out."

"Where does this come from?" Sueli asked.

"Well, it is part of the American dream. Every generation wants its kids to have a better life than it is having."

"At this rate that won't be difficult," she said.

"We are also haunted by the possibility that if, at some time later in life, our kids are underachievers, they'll forever crucify us for that one opportunity we failed to avail them of," I said. "They will say that it was the turning point, when their hopes were dashed, their dreams crushed, when things started going bad…So we better indulge them."

Sometime later the following conversation took place.

"Isabelle asked me if she can sleep over her friend's house tonight." Sueli reported. "Can't children spend a few hours having fun with each other in the park and then go back to their homes?"

"Sure, it's possible," I said. "It just never happens. The idea is that if you enjoy spending time with a friend, then more time means more enjoyment. If there's nothing pressing on the calendar, then why end the party?"

"Because it's ridiculous. I can't talk to my children as I want if their friends are there right next to them for days!," she said.

"Talk to them about what?" I asked.

"Cleaning their rooms, cleaning the kitchen, doing chores, going out," she replied.

"That's the idea. They know their friends are like a force field. While they're in our house, we can't call our girls to account." I said. "It's pure genius. It took me a while, but I figured out a work-around."

"What do you mean?" she said.

"Take Isabelle. At this point we know her close friends well enough. If she has a friend sleep over, the next morning (after they have warm bagels I've run out for) I sit both of them down. I explain that it's nothing personal, but we've got to get certain things done around the house that day. The friend has two choices: (1) Have Mom or Dad pick her up so Isabelle can get to work around the house, or (2) Work alongside Isabelle until the chores are done, at which time the party can resume. They jump at the second option! Before I know it, the friend's getting out the vacuum and bragging about how proficient she is with it. Two kids working alongside each other keeps morale high. It's like one plus one being more than two.

The work gets done in less than half the time. Bing. Bang. Boom. Done."

"You are joking!" she said. "You made Isabelle's friends do our housework?"

"No." I said. "I gave them a choice."

Our work on the former ugly duckling of a house is mostly done. The living part, the landscape, is a continuing work in progress. Something's always dying or growing out of control or just barely hanging on. We had a nice Bradford Pear tree in the front, surrounded by a big lawn. Then Irene hit. With a full set of leaves to catch the wind and the ground soaked from rain and floodwaters, the roots on the windward side just lifted out of the ground. The tree tilted over. It looked absurd. I don't know about you, but I can't live with a tilted tree. We tried using stakes and ratcheting straps and even pulling it upright with a pickup truck burning rubber in the street. It just wouldn't budge.

The tree was eventually replaced with a six-foot-tall Home Depot special, a "little tree that could" flowering cherry. With its planting came the opportunity to center it in the yard. Audrey and I named it Titanic because we planted it on the one-hundredth anniversary of the sinking of the boat. It was doing well until one night during which two loud parties were held in the neighborhood. At least one guest thought his or her night would not be complete without walking across the lawn to the tree, breaking it in half, and throwing the top part in the street. Thanks much, stranger. We've since tried planting a southern magnolia in the spot, but it just could not get out of its own way. Each spring it would form new growth that would go no-where. It's not the only magnolia in the neighborhood that is struggling. We have recently gone back to a flowering cherry, "Son of Titanic," if you will. It's doing well, but, until it gets bigger, it's vulnerable.

That there's any tree in the front of the house is a big deal. Sueli is just not partial to trees; she fears that, in a storm, they'll fall over and land on the house. The poten-tial damage to people and property keep her up at night. Touring the neighborhood after a windstorm, we have seen our share of trees that fell into houses. But it's risen to the level of phobia. If a one-hundred-foot-tall tree stood two hundred feet from the house, I am quite confident she would fear it. One day when we were talking trees, I pointed out that the large array of magnificent hardwood trees throughout our neighborhood contributed to it being so nice. "Trees" she responded, "belong in the woods."

One of the advantages of living in a four-season climate is getting the opportunity to witness the miracle of plants of all manner come alive. There's one tree that stands apart. It prefers to send up new growth from the ground as off-shoots of the current trunk. It blooms late in the summer. The blooms appear at the very ends of the branches. It's got an odd, two-word name. Care to guess? Sueli did; she said, "Finally, our Cape Murder is blooming!" A year later she took another shot, saying, "Honey, look at the beautiful white flowers on our Crepe Murple." For these moments of humor alone, living with Sueli is worth any price!

A consistent bright spot is our perennials. The tulips are just OK. The daffodils are better. Then come the spectacular peonies. Its flowers are so big, the plant can't support them. If we don't intervene, the blooms droop to the ground. All kinds of lilies come after that, followed by gladiolus that have to be seen to be believed. Planted a few seasons ago from bulbs obtained at Home Depot and Lowe's, they come firing out of the ground bigger and better each year. During the most recent season, some have reached a height of six feet. While recently working in the front corner bed, I had the pleasure of talking with a driver stopped at the stop sign. She complimented us on our flowers and said she looked forward to coming home every day and stopping at that exact spot to admire them. The transformation was complete. We'd progressed from a liability in the neighborhood to an asset.

On a hot summer day, if Sueli catches a plant wilting, she'll urge me to act, "Honey, grab the rose and throw some water on it."

Sueli takes great pleasure in seeing our plants break the soil in the spring, becoming so formidable over the next few months and producing flowers that are just magnificent. She refers to our plants in the feminine, exclaiming, "Look honey, she's going to produce another flower!" Sueli is also fiercely defensive of her flowers. Woe be to the person who inadvertently steps on one. There have been times when

I've given an honest assessment of which plants were doing well and which were a disappointment. She'd get close and produce a "Shhhh" followed by a whisper, "They need our encouragement. Don't talk that way around them!"

A few years ago, the girls began a drumbeat that became louder and bolder until one day it reached a fever pitch. What was their demand? "We want a pet!" "Oh, great," I thought. They were ready to step into parenthood. I'd grown up a dog person. I always thought that dogs were so much more straightforward than cats. The big problem with a dog, of course, is that it requires much more maintenance than a cat. I knew I could not count on the girls to be dutiful about walking a dog.

The girls named our cat Jake. He is really cool; he is very independent but a good sport when the girls pick him up and treat him like anything from a newborn to an around-the-back-of-the-neck big cat. Audrey and a friend posted a Vine of them creating a cat burrito by rolling Jake up in a small blanket. He's that chill.

We've frequently lined up the neighbor's teen daughter to check on Jake when we've planned to be gone from the house for several days. It always seems to be a last-minute thing. At some point before each trip Sueli will inquire, "Honey, did you call the walk dogger?"

Jake is in touch with his wild side. He likes to spend the entire night out, prowling the numerous beds around the house for insects, moths, and the occasional mouse. Sueli is a big advocate of Jake's freedom, likening house cats to Orcas at Sea World. The girls would prefer that he never be out. They usually lure him back in before going to sleep, but not always.

Sueli sometimes goes cat-whisperer on us. "Jake looks nervous," she observes. "Maybe he has to make a puppy." The girls counter, "Mom, it's poopy, not puppy!"

The first of us to open the front door in the morning may be startled as Jake bolts past for his food and water. That SOB is perfectly happy to be outside on the warmest of summer days to the coldest of winter nights. On the rare occasion that he wants in during the night, he'll make a racket that is impossible to miss. Now if we could only get the girls to agree on whose turn it is to clean the litter box…

Between Audrey and Isabelle, Audrey is the athlete, while Isabelle is a girly girl. Opportunities are all around us, so I have encouraged the girls to participate in sports for a season. If they like them, they can pursue sports further. But, it's been tough for Audrey to get a foothold in the athletically oriented district in which we live. She didn't grow up playing sports, so her fellow competitors have several years of experience on her. At least, because she climbed everything she could back in Brazil, Audrey has serious upper body strength. But my perspective is not shared by my significant other. Sueli has remarked that sports involve people battling each other over a ball. They will kick the ball and throw the ball and chase the ball. They will hurt each other in pursuit of the ball. When the game is over, they will stop chasing the ball. Having played a ton of ice hockey and baseball growing up, I am a firm believer in sports. I've expressed to Sueli that sports teach people valuable life lessons. For example, there is a distinct connection between the preparation a person makes for a sports competition and her performance in the competition. How is preparation for a big exam, a job interview, or performance not crucial? Then there is the need to trust in one's teammates and coaches. Teamwork happens even in individual sports. Just ask any athlete who was able to take his or her game to the next level because of a great coach or trainer.

In sports as in life, there is a slippery slope when it comes to fair play. Here and there athletes can get away with cheating. But victories through cheating are hollow, and they gnaw on anyone with a conscience. It was conscience led Marion Jones to publicly fess up about her ill-gotten Olympic running medals and feel a great relief in doing so. Conscience-driven golfers are particularly respected. They are the ones who have been known to call penalties on themselves when no one was looking.

The other compelling aspect of sports is the winning and losing. It is sobering to prepare intensely for a competition, to expend every ounce of concentration and energy on the field, and to still come up short. We have to be prepared for losses in life. No one wins every time. Sports teach us how to learn from losses, pick ourselves up, and move forward. And, just as no one likes a sore loser, no one likes a "sore winner," either. From losses comes humility. From humility comes the ability to win with grace and perspective instead of arrogance and conceit.

I touch on these themes during the year as Audrey experience ups and downs in her athletic endeavors. I often think that I see Sueli listening intently, and I begin to think that perhaps I am finally winning her over to my point of view. On these occasions, I finish what I have to say about sports and look expectantly to her for affirmation. "Sports," she'll respond, "are dumb."

It's said that humans are born with exploration genes. Not unlike many other families, we love to venture out, expand our horizons, and travel. Road-tripping and Priceline make travel easy. During one trip, we drove to Niagara Falls and spent a day there. Then it was on to Chicago for several days. On the way back, we stopped in Corning, New York, to see the Corning Company's amazing museum that is as much about light as it is glass. The whole trip consumed just one week, with no early mornings and no driving past midnight!

When it comes to finances, it seems like we're in a leaky boat. We put more money into the boat each year, but it seems to disappear. Travel surely isn't helping. Sueli wants to get a handle on it, and told me, "We have to make a budget from top to bottle to know how to make meets ends."

Over the years we've also flown and/or driven to Philadelphia, Boston, Newport, New Orleans, Las Vegas, and the Grand Canyon. We've crisscrossed the states of Arizona, Florida, and California. Sueli calls on her tour-guide background to make sure it's always an "experience." Isabelle recently announced that she wants us to visit Hawaii next.

Europe has eluded us, but we were able to get Audrey there on a school trip. Inquiring about the specifics of the trip, Sueli asked Audrey: "Are you going to French? To German?"

As an educator, I know the parents of my students play a tremendous role in their educations. A parent is my ace in the hole, the person I call when I am having a problem with a child's behavior that I cannot remedy. The vast majority of my students would choose to suffer just about any fate other than a call home to their parents. Now as a parent myself, I am keen to learn what's going on in the girls' schools and how they see things. A few times over the years, they've had run-ins with administrators over their behavior. Keep in mind that these are two of the nicest, most well-meaning girls you will find. (But aren't they all?)

Some of the most bizarre incidents had to with Isabelle and her behavior at lunch. She has been repeatedly criticized for being too loud (at lunch!). She's also been chastised and threatened over leaving her table to visit friends at another table. The topper, for sure, is her violating the rule against touching. That our best solution to some problem is to prohibit touching is a sad story we'll leave for another day.

Audrey was once called down to the dean for pulling down the shorts of another girl. The discipline for this conduct was a suspension. Audrey was miserable. Sueli was called to the school. Audrey explained that she was playing on the monkey bars when she slipped and began falling off. She instinctively grabbed at whatever was in front of her, which happened to be the other girl. Audrey said that she apologized to the girl right after it happened and that the girl accepted her apology. It must have been un-accepted sometime later. After listening to Audrey's explanation and the administrators' careful dissertation on the serious consequences of Audrey's behavior, Sueli paused for a moment to gather her thoughts. When she eventually did open her mouth, she proceeded to dress down the administrators for making Audrey miserable with their threats and for wasting her time with their stupidity. She left. The administrators were aghast. Audrey was not suspended. Somehow, despite the lack of serious discipline for her horrific behavior, she's managed to have a clean record devoid of any shorts-pulling ever since.

Sueli recounted the meeting later that day. About the dean she said that she was simply not going to "lick his ass." "The expression," I responded, "is 'kiss his ass.'" She asked, "What's the difference?"

Some years later Audrey was called out of class and down to the dean, for what she did not know. The dean explained to her that her attire was unacceptable. She would have to cover up. She looked down at what she was wearing. It was winter. She had on a sweater and jeans. No part of her body was exposed. She pointed this out to the dean and suggested that maybe it would be best to call her mom. The dean thought about that prospect and sent Audrey back to class—with no change in her attire—a few moments later.

Years into our marriage, Sueli's language foibles are fewer but no less endearing to me. Of my mentally sharp parents, she has said, "I am so happy they are not getting Alzmeirs." On the possibility of Audrey earning some money, she has asked, "Audrey, why don't you try to get a job as a baby city?" On wanting to do something about the excessive accumulation of things around the house, she will exclaim, "We have to clean up this cluster!"

She and I are still going one hundred miles per hour, pursuing this project and that while dutifully serving as parents. We've yet to get in sync with a housecleaner. Sueli can typically be heard to say, "The bathroom is a mess. This weekend let's clean the bathtube."

Each day that I delay sending this work to editing promises to yield another story. Acting on her desire to see our house cleaned up, she again looked around for a person who shared her commitment to hard work. The other day a Brazilian mom-and-daughter team came over to see the house and learn what Sueli wanted them to do. Sueli had coffee and pastries ready. A few hours later, they left. I asked if she'd decided to use their services. She laughed and admitted that they got so busy talking about life, they never did get around to talking business.

The ladies eventually came to the house. Sueli worked alongside them. When I returned home later that day, I thought I was dreaming. The place was immaculate. There was a place for everything, and everything was in its place. For me, it was pure bliss, and I wondered, "Why didn't we do it sooner?" The next day I opened the attic door in search of something and was nearly knocked over by a collapsing wall of all the crap they had stuffed in there.

Sueli's unintended ability to combine the tragic with the hilarious is priceless. Summarizing a recent headline-grabbing story for me, she said, "This man returned to the house of his former girlfriend. When she opened the door, he pulled out a gun and blow her out." Even after she speaks perfect English, it's impossible to predict what will come out of her mouth next. Her straightforward Brazilian sensibility is a welcome complement to my overly measured approach to life.

It is hard to believe that when I first met the girls, they were little buggers whom I tossed around with abandon. They embraced me fearlessly. When they arrived, things weren't so complicated. They made friends easily; they had playdates. But once each one entered double-digits in age, allegiances shifted, priorities changed, and it became more difficult for them to find their place among other girls.

Despite the headwinds, the girls are transforming into women. We are turning our attention to things like working papers and driver's licenses. We talk about what careers they will pursue and in which country they will attend college. Will they ultimately want to live here in the United States or in Brazil? Sueli and I wonder the same about ourselves.

Years ago Sueli gave up everything to bring herself and her girls to the United States so that they could have the benefit of being raised with a father. I've never lost sight of this, and I work hard so that at the end of every day, she still concludes that she made the right decision.

My dear wife recently approached me, saying, "You've got a birthday coming up. What can I get you that will be special?" I responded with the only thing that was missing from my life: "A set of sheets."

The Billboard may have ended, but the adventures of Tom, Sueli, Audrey, Isabelle and their cat Jake continue. Keep up with them at https://www.facebook.com/TheBillboardBook.